Smiling Inside, Smiling Outside

Learning to care for myself, my family, my world

Susanna Palomares

Published by

Brilliant Publications
1 Church View
Sparrow Hall Farm
Edlesborough
Dunstable
Bedfordshire LU6 2ES

Sales and stock enquiries:
Tel: 01202 712910
Fax: 0845 1309300
e-mail:brilliant@bebc.co.uk
www.brilliantpublications.co.uk
General information enquiries:
Tel: 01525 229720

The name 'Brilliant Publications' and the
logo are registered trade marks.

Cover illustration:
Lynda Murray
Illustrations: Roger Johnson
Copyright © 1993, Innerchoice Publishing
P.O. Box 2476, Spring Valley, California,
91979, USA

ISBN: 1 903853 737
Reprinted 2005 in the UK by
Lightning Source
10 9 8   7 6 5 4 3 2 1

Contents

Introduction

Welcome and enjoy

Smiling Inside,
Smiling Outside

Day in and day out, experience by experience, young children pursue a continuous process of organizing and framing their concepts and comprehensions of themselves and, based on these perceptions, their relative self-esteem. They want to know who they are, what they can do, and what powers they have to affect their world.

If you have worked for any length of time with very young children, either as a teacher, counsellor, or parent of youngsters in the early years and primary, and are always searching for activities with which to aid and abet the mission of these eager young learners, *Smiling Inside, Smiling Outside* is for you.

It is your resource, filled cover to cover with rich experiences that you can grasp at a glance and use immediately, with minimal preparation.

The goal of *Smiling Inside, Smiling Outside* is to develop in children positive perceptions of themselves and their place in the world. The activities, which are arranged by theme area, are designed to help children:

- cultivate positive esteem and self-awareness
- learn to value family and community connections and develop a sense of belonging
- work collaboratively, with consideration for others
- focus on listening, speaking, and writing – important aspects of communication
- develop feelings of wonder and appreciation for the natural world.

Like a partially cut gem, each activity is small and succinct, and waiting to be further shaped, developed, and embellished by you. You know your children better than anyone, and are encouraged to modify the activities to suit their interests, ages, languages, cultures, and learning abilities.

The activities are arranged in a logical order, progressing from a focus on 'me' to a concern for 'my world'. Within any one theme area, certain clusters of activities may be arranged in sequential order, each activity building on the concepts and skills of the previous activity. You will recognize such groupings when you see them.

Beyond these considerations, the activities in *Smiling Inside, Smiling Outside* may be used flexibly and in any order you choose.

While all of the activities in this collection are designed to be implemented with groups of children, they may be readily adapted for use with one or two youngsters. As such, *Smiling Inside, Smiling Outside* is an excellent resource for both formal and informal efforts at home schooling.

Young children don't usually respond well to heavy doses of cognition. They want to observe, explore, touch, smell, taste, manipulate, talk, sing, dance, and then move on to something else. As much as possible, allow your children this kind of freedom. However, do maintain a rich dialogue with the children about what they are learning. Encourage them to talk about their experiences, and to ask any questions generated by those experiences.

Many of the activities in *Smiling Inside, Smiling Outside* will open avenues to new areas of interest. Notice sparks of enthusiasm and curiosity, and expand learning in these areas by developing additional activities, reading related literature, performing role plays, creating works of art, and visiting places in the community. The possibilities in any area are virtually endless. Above all, let the children experience and enjoy, and trust that learning will follow.

1

Learning about me

The activities in this section help you develop positive esteem and self-awareness in your students. These non-threatening and fun experiences encourage children to become aware of themselves relative to a number of different dimensions.

Watch us grow

This activity should be initiated at the beginning and continued throughout the year. It will give the children many opportunities to recognize and acknowledge their physical growth, as well as acquaint them with record-keeping and measurement techniques. Tape a length of paper (marked off in centimetre units to at least one and a half metres tall) vertically on a wall or door. At the beginning of the year, have each child stand in bare feet with his/her back against the paper. Keep a chart giving each child's name, recorded height and date. Give new children entering the class an opportunity to be measured, too. Repeat this exercise every couple of months throughout the year.

At the end of the year, after you have measured growth several times, take a large sheet of chart paper and draw a vertical column for each child, plus one extra column. In the first column, mark off in 5cm units. Read off the first series of recorded measurements, have one child at a time fill in his/her column with a colour, up to the point of the first measurement (e.g., from the bottom of the column to 110cm); then with a different colour to the point of the second measurement (e.g., from 110cm to 116cm); and then with a third colour to the point of the third measurement (e.g., from 116cm to 120cm) and so on. Finally, help the children measure each other for a final time and, with a different coloured crayon, have them extend their column by colouring up to their current height. Talk about how much the children have grown, and encourage a class discussion about growth. Have the children write down their measurement dates and heights on a piece of paper, and take this growth report home.

Classroom suggestion box

This activity encourages children to observe and make decisions concerning their participation in the classroom, and enables you to get to know their ideas and desires.

Provide a box into which the children can put their ideas. Invite them to submit ideas concerning how the room could be made to look and feel new or different, and about activities in which they would like to be involved. Set aside time on a regular basis to review the suggestions and discuss them with the children. Acknowledge all ideas and keep an ongoing list of suggestions. Try to use as many as possible. For very young children, set aside a time when you can listen as they express their ideas. Record their suggestions.

Birthday acknowledgements

At the beginning of the school year, create a special birthday storyboard. On separate lengths of sugar paper, write the name, birthday, and a positive statement about each child. Take photographs of the children to place on their story-boards (or have them bring in photographs). Arrange the completed stories in chronological order in a box, and then put each child's story on the bulletin board during the appropriate month. Make sure to acknowledge those children who have summer birthdays. July would be a good month to put up the stories of all children born during summer months.

Tyler Roger's birthday is on 22nd October. Tyler has big brown eyes, is friendly to everyone and likes to play football and read comic books.

Say 'cheese'

Tell the children that you are going to take pictures of them, and that you would like each of them to select a special place for the photograph to be taken. Explain that the setting for the photo can be either indoors or outdoors, but that you want the children to think carefully before selecting the perfect spot for their picture. Use either Polaroid or regular film, both have advantages. With Polaroid, you can complete the entire activity in a single session or, on the other hand, waiting a few days for the photos to be developed is exciting, and permits you to extend the activity to another day.

After the photos have been developed, mount them on single sheets of sugar paper and have the children embellish their pictures with a fancy signature. Put the sheets into plastic wallets in a ring binder and keep it in a location where the children can enjoy it as often as they wish.

Or you could ...
Take the photographs and display them on the walls or bulletin board. Look at the pictures with the children, and discuss any similarities or differences they observe in the pictures. Make a list of the children's observations on chart paper.

Ask the children to stand in a large circle facing one another. Ask the following questions to help sharpen the children's awareness of characteristics that people have in common:

- Is there anyone in the room who looks exactly like you?
- In what way is everyone you see like you?
- What do all of the children have that you have?

Encourage discussion regarding similarities. Help the children develop an understanding of characteristics that all humans share.

What I like

Provide old magazines and ask the children to look through them and cut out pictures of the following:

- something beautiful
- their favourite colour
- something funny
- a favourite food
- something sad
- something happy.

Have the children paste these cutouts on coloured sugar paper. Ask them to write or dictate their names and why they chose the things that they cut out. Combine all the papers and make a class book. Invite the children to suggest cover designs and to become involved in creating the cover.

Happiness pictures and words

Provide magazines and scissors, and have the children find and cut out pictures of things that give them a happy feeling. Next, ask the children to name some of the feelings elicited by the pictures while you list the words on a large piece of paper. Then, have the children look through the magazines again to see how many of these happiness words they can find and cut out. Finally, have the children glue all of the cut-out pictures and words onto the paper so that they surround the happiness word list.

A personal exhibit

The children can make exhibits about themselves on a display panel made of three pieces of cardboard taped together so that it will stand when folded. Have the children write their name in large letters across the top of the centre panel. Ask the children to collect items of all sorts that tell something about themselves. Suggest that they use photos, drawings, postcards, ribbons, awards, pictures from magazines that are meaningful to them – even an object from when they were babies. They can use anything at all that helps to describe who they are. Encourage thought and creativity.

When the exhibits are complete, display them around the room and have the children take turns talking about the items in their display.

Save the display cards and set them up again on parents' evening.

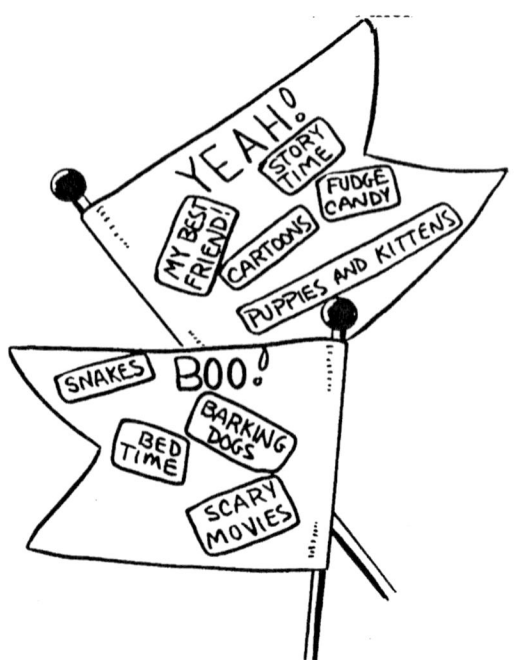

Yeah! Boo!

Begin this activity by facilitating a discussion about things that the children like and dislike. Accept all comments without judgement. Have the children make two banners each by gluing or taping sugar paper around two straws. At the top of one banner, have the children write *Yeah!* At the top of the other, *Boo!* Ask the children to write down the names of everything they can think of that they like on the *Yeah!* banner and everything they dislike on the *Boo!* banner.

14

Performing shadows

Help the children learn about their bodies and how they move and use them by experimenting with and controlling their shadows to perform different actions. Set up a good source of light for casting shadows. Suggest actions involving different parts of the body, and have the children make their shadows perform those actions. For example, suggest that the performing child make his/her shadow raise its arms; bend its right elbow; raise its left leg; hop, jump, bend, and curl its body. Ask the children to think of actions which their shadows cannot do. Try them out. Have the children experiment with both profiles and front views.

Silhouettes

Heighten each child's sense of self-awareness by creating a silhouette of him or her. Tape a sheet of black sugar paper to the wall. With a child sitting between a projector (or a lamp, if no projector is available) and the taped paper, draw the child's silhouette as it is projected on the paper. Cut out the silhouette, mount it, and write the child's name on the back. Display the silhouettes around the room. Give the children an opportunity to go around the room and identify the various silhouettes. Allow collaboration during the identification process.

Painting faces

How to make face paint:
Mix a few drops of food colouring into a small amount of petroleum jelly.

or

Add a few drops of water to watercolour paints.

Suggest that the children can be clowns, kittens, birds, monsters, old people.

Ask the children to decide who or what they would like to be. Have the children form pairs and paint their partner's face to represent the character their partner wants to be.

After all the faces are painted, have the children write a story about their character.

Try having the children spend the entire day 'in character'. If you do this, you might want to monitor what characters the children choose (a monster could prove a bit of a distraction). At the end of the day, debrief the children concerning what it was like to experience the world as someone or something else.

Look at me

Provide a large mirror (a full-size dressing mirror if possible), and ask the children to stand in front of it, one at a time. Ask the class to gather around and to find as many ways as possible to describe how the mirrored child looks ('Jane has a happy smile' or 'Manuel has thick black hair'). Use the mirror exercise as an opportunity to compliment the children ('Maria is wearing such a pretty dress'), to encourage good grooming ('Look how neat Jim's hair is'), and to point out similarities and differences ('Henry and Hamid both have brown eyes' or 'Sally is shorter than Katie'). Make sure that every child gets a turn in front of the mirror, and that each receives positive feedback.

As a follow-up to this activity, have every child do a self-portrait. Encourage the children to return to the mirror for another look as they complete their pictures. When the self-portraits are finished, ask the children to remember a positive statement made about them during the mirror exercise, and write that statement on their self-portrait. Be sure to include their names. For example: 'Jack has sparkling white teeth.'

17

The magic chair

Receiving positive feedback from others is one way children develop a positive self-image. The following activity can be used regularly throughout the year. Make sure all of the children have equal opportunities to sit in the 'Magic Chair'.

Completely cover a small chair with pieces of shiny aluminum foil. Tape a sign reading 'Magic Chair' to the back. Ask the class to sit in a semi-circle on the floor in front of the chair while a child sits in the chair. Tell the children that when they sit inside the Magic Circle, they will hear lots of wonderful and positive things about themselves. Then, ask one classmate at a time to say something nice to the child who is sitting in the chair – a positive observation, an admired quality, or an attractive feature. Take your turn first during the first few Magic Chair sessions so that you can model appropriate comments and observations.

18

The feelings game

Help your children to develop an understanding of the roles of body language and facial expression in the communication of feelings by playing this feelings-pantomime game. Use the list of feelings words to make a large chart divided into squares with one word in each square. Provide a small object such as a jack or stone. Either one at a time or in pairs, ask the children to throw the stone so that it lands on one of the squares. Do this privately, so the rest of the class doesn't see where the stone lands. Direct the children to take a few moments to plan a short pantomime demonstrating their feelings word. Explain that they are to act only with their faces and bodies. They may not say words or make noises. The objective is to do such an accurate pantomime that the class can identify the feeling. Enjoy and clap after each pantomime. Then ask the rest of the class to name the feeling that was demonstrated.

'Feeling' words

happy	bad	friendly
jealous	proud	beautiful
good	lazy	angry
brave	guilty	left out
scared	confused	helpful
loveable	lonely	comfortable
homesick	loving	sad
horrible	peaceful	nervous
excited	ignored	quiet
afraid	tired	powerful
relaxed	shy	silly
stupid	sleepy	wonderful
worried	grumpy	disappointed

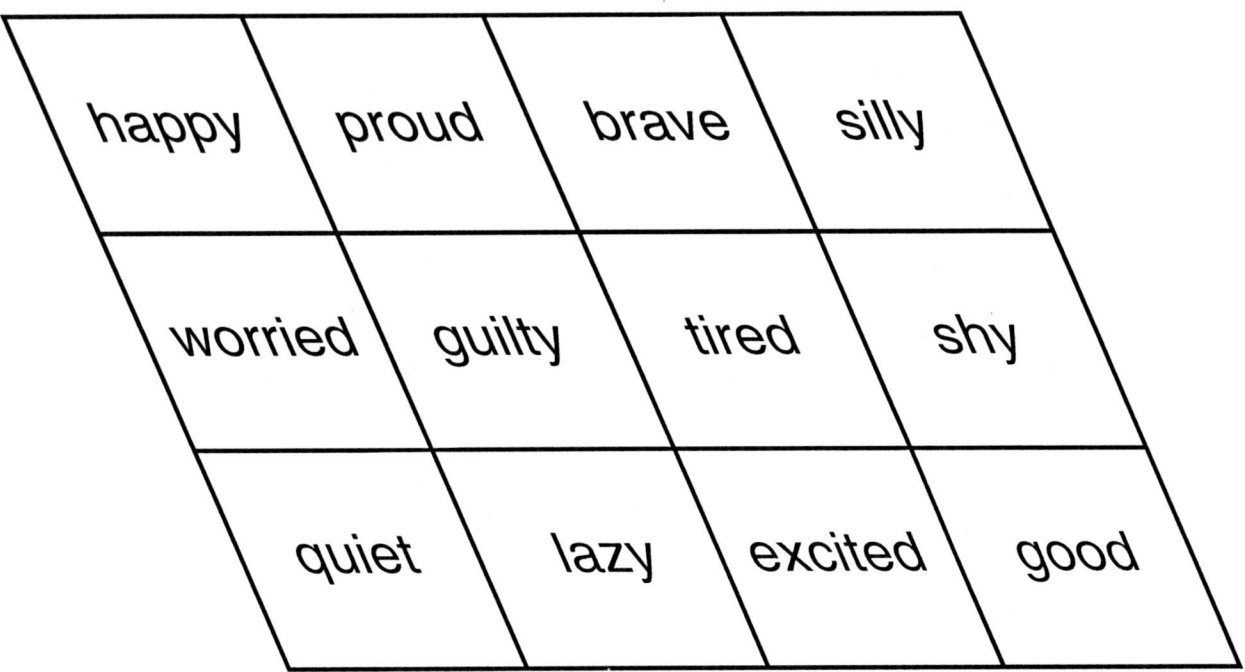

happy	proud	brave	silly
worried	guilty	tired	shy
quiet	lazy	excited	good

Taping yourself seriously

Tape record the voices of the children when they are engaged in a lively activity and unaware of what you are doing. Afterwards, play the recording back. Ask the children to listen carefully to see if they can recognize whose voice is playing on the tape. Invite them to call out when they hear their own voice. If a child doesn't immediately recognize his/her own voice, others may call out the name of the child. At a later time, you may wish to re-record the voices of the children when they *know* what you are doing. See if voice recognition is any easier under these circumstances.

20

Walk with feeling

Help the children understand moods, and how moods can be expressed in movement. Ask the children why people don't always walk in the same way. Have them spread out so that they have plenty of room to move about, and encourage them to do the following: walk proud, walk happy, walk sad, walk tall, walk brave, walk scared, walk shy, walk excited, walk tired. Next, ask them to pretend to do the following: walk in a river, walk in deep snow, walk through caves, walk up a hill, down a hill, walk in a puddle, walk through the jungle.

The magic pencil

Discuss with the children the meaning of the saying 'getting something off your chest'. Give each child a new, sharpened pencil to which you have attached a brightly coloured ribbon near the unsharpened end. Ask the children to pretend that the pencil is magic. Tell them that they may write whatever they wish with the pencil – especially if they want to 'get something off their chest'. You may want to provide brightly coloured stationery for the children to write on.

21

The wishing well

Make a copy of the wishing well on the next page. Make multiple copies of the coins or draw your own. Cut out the wishing well. Fold and tape the well along the seam so that it is free-standing.

Introduce the activity by asking if any of the children has ever thrown a coin into a wishing well. Talk about the purpose of a wishing well, and explain that a person usually tosses a coin into the well while making a silent wish, but today we're going to make our wishes and then talk about them.

Give one coin to each child. Have the children write the name of something they wish for on the coin. If necessary, have them whisper their wish to you, or an assistant, who then writes it down. One at a time, have the children put their coins into the wishing well while explaining to the class what they wished for. Place a container of additional coins near the well so that when the children think of other wishes they may drop other coins into the well. Children may volunteer to help make someone's wish come true. Be sure to take your turn at the well.

My family and community

This unit is designed to help children learn to value family and community connections. Knowing more about family relations and how individuals co-operate and contribute to the family helps children develop a sense of belonging and esteem. These benefits are further strengthened when children recognize how individuals and families collaborate to build and sustain functioning communities that serve everyone.

My family

Have the children identify each member of their family, and then draw a picture showing the entire family, including themselves. Have them write a short caption beneath each family member's likeness, identifying specific contributions that person makes to the household. Does he or she ...work at home? ...away from home? ...do outside chores? ...cook meals? ...wash dishes? What does each child do to help the family? On the back of their picture, have the children list things which they can do personally to help other members of their family. (Very young children can represent their ideas with additional small drawings.)

26

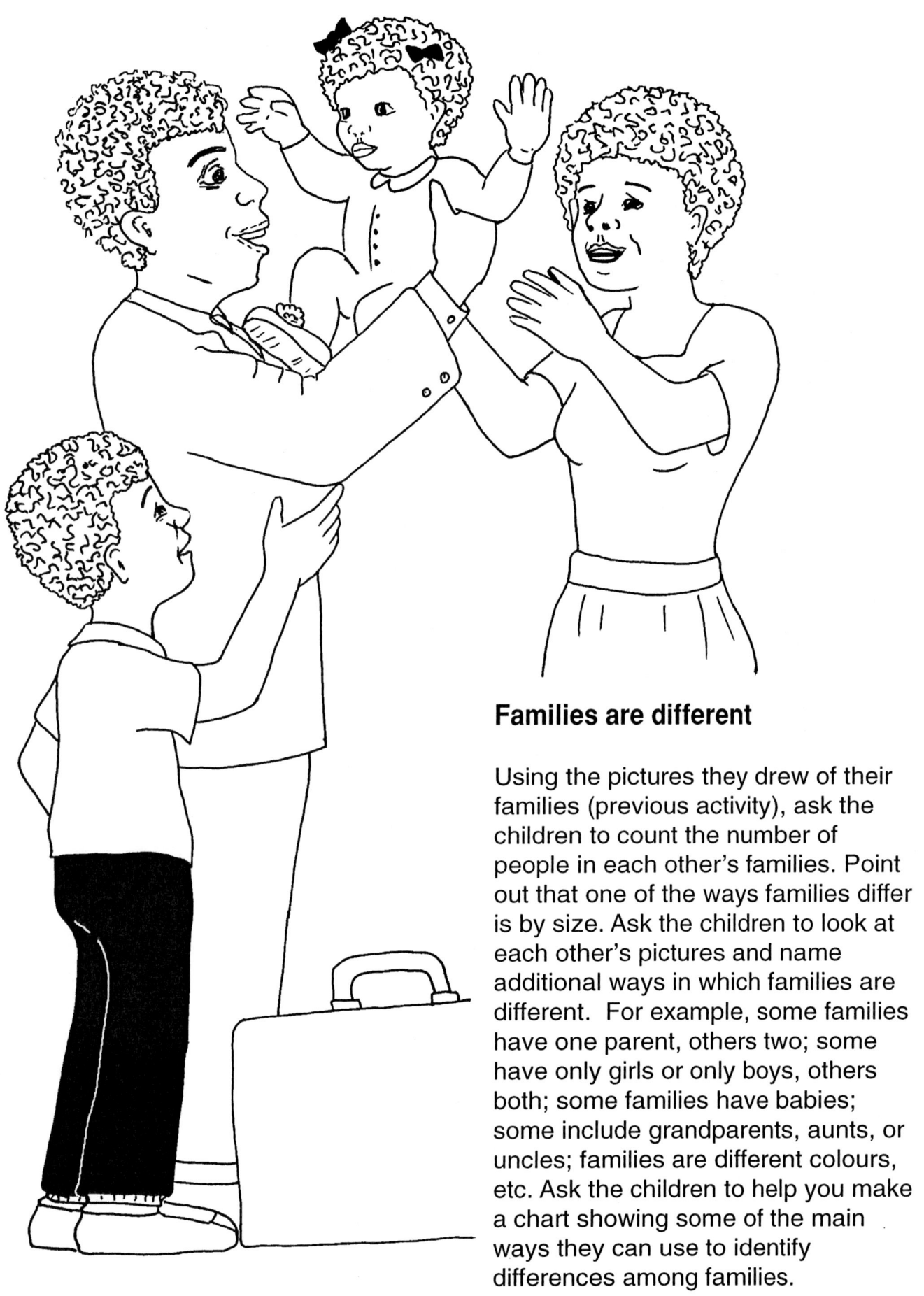

Families are different

Using the pictures they drew of their families (previous activity), ask the children to count the number of people in each other's families. Point out that one of the ways families differ is by size. Ask the children to look at each other's pictures and name additional ways in which families are different. For example, some families have one parent, others two; some have only girls or only boys, others both; some families have babies; some include grandparents, aunts, or uncles; families are different colours, etc. Ask the children to help you make a chart showing some of the main ways they can use to identify differences among families.

Drawing conclusions

Read aloud one or both of the following story starters and have the children draw a picture of the conclusion they would choose. When the drawings are finished, invite the children to tell the class something about them. Encourage discussion about the real meaning of gift giving.

'Once upon a time there was a very young boy who wanted to give his mother a special birthday gift, but he had no money – not even a penny. This boy didn't know anyone who had any money, and he wasn't old enough to get a job. He was very worried that he wouldn't have a gift for his mother. Then two days before his mother's birthday, he thought of something to give her. What was it?'

'Pretend that it is almost Christmas and your parents tell you that they don't want you to buy a gift for them. Instead, they want you to do something special for them. What might that something special be?'

Play house

Bring in several large cardboard packing boxes such as the ones refrigerators or washing machines come in. Cut windows and doors. Provide art materials so that the children can paint their 'houses'. Suggest that they hang pictures they have created, and make curtains of cloth scraps. Carpet samples and pillows can be placed on the floor. Discuss activities that go on in their own homes, and encourage the children to dramatize these same activities in their play houses.

We all come from somewhere

Have your children ask their parents and/or grandparents where they were born. Ask them to find out if they have always lived in the same area or if they came from another country, or if they moved here from another part of the country.

Some things for the children to learn from their parents and/or grandparents are: What is it like to leave one's home and go where you don't know anyone or what to expect? What things are the same in both countries/regions and what things are different? What problems do people have when they move to a new home? (For very young children, you may want to send a letter home explaining the nature of this activity, and listing the questions you would like the parents and/or grandparents to answer.) Finally, invite some of the parents/grandparents to your class to share their experiences.

Demonstrate using a globe and maps to show the children the various places they have talked about in the course of sharing their parents/ grandparents travels. Help the children to gain an awareness of the distances involved. Talk about the different modes of transportation used, and emphasize the differences between travel today and travel in earlier times.

Create a classroom chart showing how many different counties and/or countries are represented in the class. Make sure that the names of all children are included on the chart.

Read a story* about the problems encountered when one moves. After the story compile a list with the children of the problems of moving to a new place. The move can be to a new neighbourhood, community, or country.

*Let's Move Together Carol M. Schubeck (The Suitcase Press, 2000) We're Moving House Heather Maisner (Kingfisher Books, 1997)

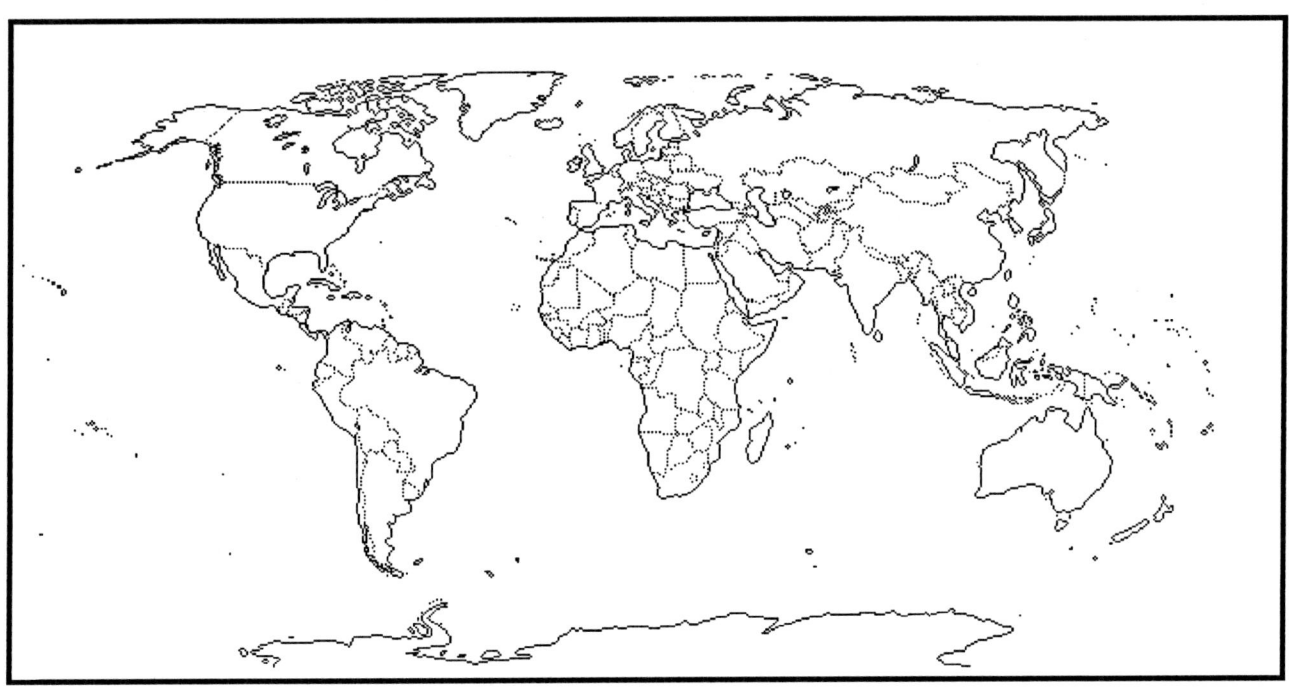

Our school neighbourhood

Initiate a discussion by asking the children, 'Who lives and works in the neighbourhood around our school?' As the children recall people, list names, labels, or descriptions on the board or on paper. Encourage the children to think of the different types of shop in your area (supermarket, clothes, chemist, post office, etc.) along with firefighters, police officers, friends, and neighbours. If the children fail to include the school and its employees, remind them that these buildings and the people in them are part of the neighbourhood, too. If possible, take a walk around the neighbourhood. Point out buildings, shops, and streets, and ask questions like, 'Who lives there?' and 'Who works in that shop?'

Make a class mural of the school neighbourhood by attaching a long role of paper to one classroom wall (white lining paper works perfectly). Help the children decide who will be responsible for the various parts of the mural. Make sure all of the children have a part in the mural's creation. Continue the discussion of the neighbourhood and its people as the children work. Help everyone understand that the people who live and work in the area are important, and that they share responsibility for creating a co-operative neighbourhood.

What people need

Have the children compile a list of all the different kinds of facilities they illustrated on their school neighbourhood mural. When the school neighbourhood list is complete, ask the children to name other kinds of facilities in your community that are outside the immediate area of the school. The complete list should include things such as shops, homes, parks, garages, other businesses, churches/temples, fire stations, hospitals, leisure centres, etc. As the children name facilities, write them on the board. When the list is complete, read each item and ask the children,'Does your family need this?' and 'Can they survive without it?' Encourage discussion about what true needs are. Help the children understand that food, clothing, and shelter are basic needs.

Who works at our school?

Ask the children who works at their school besides their teachers. Help them to name as many positions as possible, including head teacher, secretaries, caretakers, social workers, counsellors, teaching assistants, canteen staff, nurse, etc. Take a tour of the school to see the school workers engaged in their activities. Check with several workers beforehand and identify four or five who would be willing to tell the children what they do in their jobs. When you return to the classroom, discuss the different duties that the children observed being performed.

Help the children to understand that everyone in the school has an important function and that, in order for the school to run smoothly, all workers must co-operate and contribute to the school's success. Have the children work together and make a big floor plan of the school using building blocks. The plan doesn't need to be accurate, merely representative of all the places visited by the children when they took their school tour. Encourage the children to role-play the different school workers they observed and talked with. Use the block floor plan as a prop.

Who supplies our basic needs?

Help the children to develop an understanding of the things people need to live, and how they co-operate with each other to provide society with basic products and services.

On the board, write the headings Food, Clothing, and Shelter. Ask the children if they know who supplies people with these things. Encourage the children to figure out where the basic necessities of life come from by asking questions such as, 'Where does your family get food?' 'Where do supermarkets get food?' If any of the children's parents are involved in supplying these needs, talk about what these individuals do and their importance in the chain. As the children develop a picture of the flow of goods and services, create a list under each heading. It might look something like the table below.

Bring in old magazines and have the children find and cut out pictures of people at work. Paste the pictures on coloured paper. Discuss with the children the types of work taking place in the various pictures. Does the work represent a service their family uses? Label each picture with a caption suggested by the children. Display the pictures around the room.

Food	Clothing	Shelter
Supermarket	Shop	Builders
Packing plant	Factory	Materials suppliers
Farms	Plants and animal	Forests

Something I want

Ask the children to keep a record of all the goods and services their family uses for a two-day period. Make a class chart of all the goods and services used by all of the families.

Make a list of as many occupations as the children can name related to the goods and services used by their families.

Invite parents to come in and share information about their jobs. Ask them to describe the parts they contribute to obtaining basic needs for the community.

Have the children draw a picture of something they really, really want. The subject of their drawing needn't be a basic need, just something that *they feel* they cannot live without. After everyone has completed a drawing, have each child take a turn to share his/her picture and explain what it is about.

Communicating with others

Some of the most important skills children can learn are those that relate to effective communication. Individuals who listen accurately, speak effectively, and write well have greater control over themselves and greater influence in dealing with others. This unit is designed to help children focus on the listening, speaking, and writing aspects of communication as well as the general traits of being thoughtful and considerate of others.

Listen

Have the children sit quietly and listen to all the sounds around them. After several minutes of quiet listening, ask them to name as many sounds as possible that they have heard. Make a list. Next, take the children outdoors and repeat the experience.

Ask the children to reproduce the sounds they heard. First, have them reproduce the sounds with their voices and then with rhythmic instruments. Ask them if they can think of words to describe the sounds they are making (loud, soft, clicky, humming, etc.).

Make a list of the sound words they come up with. Write a group story using these sound words.

An alternative method of creating a story is to go around the class and ask each child to contribute one word. To elicit more words, go around several times. Use a tape recorder to record the story as it develops. Play back the completed story and discuss the results. Do the sentences have meaning? If not, what's wrong and how can the story be improved? Help the children understand that in order to add a word that makes sense they must listen to the words that come before.

34

Make a noise

Fill a box with items that make a variety of noises (e.g. marbles in a tin, beans in a small box, sound blocks, a whistle, a clock, etc.) Have all of the children close their eyes and put their heads down. Ask one child to take an item from the noise box and create a sound with it. Without looking, have the rest of the class try to guess the identity of the item. If the class is unable to guess correctly, ask the child who made the noise to give descriptive clues. Encourage the children to discuss what the noise sounded like. The child who correctly identifies the item

becomes the next 'noise-maker'. Ask the children to find or make something at home that produces a distinctive sound. Ask them to bring in their item the next day. Have one child at a time beat out a rhythm with his/her 'sound machine'. Then, have the other children produce the same rhythm with their sound machines. After the children have had an opportunity to mimic several different rhythm patterns, switch to having them beat out the rhythm of familiar songs.

A sound mobile

Have the children make a 'sound mobile' by collecting pictures of machines and other things that make lots of noise. Mount each picture on cardboard. Punch a hole in the top centre of the picture, put string through the hole and knot one end. Suspend the pictures on varying lengths of string from coat hangers. Hang the mobiles from the ceiling. Adapt the activity to quiet sounds, and have the children make 'quiet mobiles'.

Guess the sound

Place in a small box a number of articles that make a distinctive sound. Have one child at a time select an object and take it behind a sheet or other visual block. Concealed from view, have the child produce a noise by shaking the object, dropping it, playing it, or otherwise manipulating it. Ask the rest of the children to guess what the object is.

The sound of numbers

Auditory perception is one of the needed ingredients in listening skills. The following series of activities helps to sharpen this ability.

You will need eight marbles and a box for this activity. Count the marbles with the children as you place them in the box, one at a time. Cover the box and shake it, directing the children to listen to the sound that is produced. Have the children close their eyes while you remove several marbles from the box. Cover and shake the box again. Ask the children, 'Are there more or fewer marbles in the box now?' For fun, see if the children can guess the number of marbles in the box. Open the box and count the marbles. Continue the activity by varying the number of marbles in the box.

Provide a box and eight marbles for each child. Have the children work in pairs – A and B (or some other designation). Have the As close their eyes while the Bs put some or all of their marbles into their box and then shake it. The As listen, and then put into their box the number of marbles they estimate will make the same sound. The As shake their box and compare their sound to the sound of their partner's. The As add or subtract marbles until the sound they produce matches the Bs sound as closely as possible. The partners then open their boxes and compare numbers. Ask the partners to switch roles so that every child has at least one turn guessing and one turn matching.

For this activity, you will need eight boxes and 36 marbles. Put one marble in one box, two in another, three in another, and so on. Write the number of marbles in each box on the bottom. Mix up the order of the boxes. Then, shake the boxes and ask the children to guess the number of marbles in each box.

Bring in the clowns

This activity emphasizes listening skills, comprehension, and following directions. Provide crayons and paper. Ask the children to listen very carefully to the directions you give, and to do just what you tell them to do. (You may repeat each direction.)

1. Draw a large oval in the centre of your paper.
2. Draw three small circles in a row down the middle of the big oval.
3. Draw a circle above the oval and make it touch the oval.
4. Draw a triangle above the circle and make one flat side touch the circle.
5. Draw a tiny circle above the triangle and make it touch the triangle.
6. Draw a long oval shape touching the left side of the big oval near the top.
7. Draw a hand on the end of this long oval shape.
8. Draw a long oval shape touching the right side of the big oval near the top.
9. Draw a hand on the end of this long oval shape.
10. Draw two long oval shapes under the big oval and make them touch the big oval.
11. Draw big shoes on the ends of these two long oval shapes.

What have you drawn? Draw a face on your clown, and colour him bright colours.

42

Guess what it is

Help the children to develop effective communication skills related to questioning and problem solving. Bring in a box and several objects. Place an object in the box, and invite the children to ask questions in an effort to determine what the item is. Be sure to answer each question. After a variety of questions have been asked and answered, reveal the object. Discuss the types of questions that were asked, identifying those that moved the children towards an accurate identification of the object. Repeat the game several times, using different objects.

Bring in an item that the children are unlikely to recognize; for example, a candle snuffer, a loofah sponge, or a special animal-grooming tool. Show the object to the children, and ask them what they would like to know about it to help them guess its purpose. Help them to phrase their questions appropriately, and record their questions on paper. After a number of questions have been asked and recorded, identify the object and, if possible, demonstrate its use. Finally, re-read the questions and ask the children to help you determine which ones did not apply to the object and which ones did.

Practice in oral communication

Talk with the children about how important it is for people to communicate clearly and accurately. Discuss situations in which what a person says and how she or he says it are very important. For example, giving directions is extremely important when communication occurs between air-traffic controllers and pilots, or between a coach and the football team.

Set up an obstacle course in the class or in the school grounds, using a variety of moveable item – chairs, toys, books, wastepaper bins, etc.

Blindfold one child and spin him/her around at one end of the obstacle course. Pretend that this child is the pilot, and must land the plane in a terrible storm, without being able to see the runway. Station another child at the other end of the runway. This child plays the air-traffic controller, and must direct the pilot through the obstacle-course runway safely. Explain that if the pilot touches anything, it is considered a crash and two new children take a turn. If possible, give all of the children an opportunity to play both roles. Conclude the activity with a discussion focusing on what the children learned about communication.

We get messages

Help the children become more aware of the many ways we communicate with others. Discuss such methods as letters, telephones, mobiles, e-mails, computers, TVs, radios, magazines, books, films, and conversations. Play a communication game. Provide a number of objects that can be used to communicate, such as a drum, whistle, flag, telephone, and ball. Remember that any two items can be clapped together to make a sound, including hands. Have the children form groups of five or six. Whisper a message to one group ('I'm cold,' 'I'm lost,' 'Come out and play,' etc.). Direct the children in that group to quietly plan a way of using the props to deliver the message to the remainder of the groups. They may deliver the message as a team, or take turns delivering different parts of the message using one prop at a time. Have the other groups guess the content of the message.

Experiment with wordless communication. Give verbal directions to the children and have them demonstrate ways of giving the same directions without speaking. Some examples are: Come here! Go away! Stop! Sit! Crouch down! Be quiet! Hurry up! Turn around! Stand up! Have the children take turns being the leader. Stress that they cannot speak; instead they must use sign language to convey directions. Have the class watch and interpret silently, and then carry out each direction without saying a word. Have the leader tell the children when they have interpreted correctly.

Sharing greetings

Bring in a selection of old greetings cards. Begin the activity by asking the children to describe how they feel when they get a birthday card, get well card, valentine's card, or Christmas card. Ask, 'How do you think other people feel when they receive a card from you? Why?' Tell the children that you would like to share with them some of the cards that you have received from others. On a large sheet of paper, label a column for each type of card (e.g., get well message, birthday greeting, valentine's card, Christmas card).

Read each card, and ask the children to decide in which column the card belongs. Tape the card in the correct column. Then, ask the children which cards they like best. Finally, have the children name words that they'd like to include in a greeting sent by them to someone else. List the words on the board or on chart paper.

Sending greetings

Ask the children to think of a special person (family member, friend, neighbour, etc.) whom they would like to surprise with a greetings card. Give each child a piece of sturdy paper. Have the children fold their paper in half and draw a picture on the front. Then assist them in writing or dictating a message for the inside. Suggest that the children refer to the list of words that they most liked from the commercial greetings cards you brought in. Encourage the children to hand deliver their greetings cards.

Note: These are excellent activities for the holidays or Valentine's Day, when cards are traditionally given and received.

Write the names of children from another class on paper strips. Have each of your children select a strip, and create a card for that child. Help the children compose messages for their cards. Show them how to make envelopes using manila paper, and have each child address his/her envelope with the name selected. Ask one child to deliver the envelopes to the other classroom.

Find out the first names of children in a local hospital. Distribute the names to your class, and have each child create and address a card and envelope for one young patient. Ask the class to dictate a covering letter to the manager of the hospital requesting that the handmade cards be delivered to the children. Place all the cards in a large envelope and have the children watch as you address it. (In order to make sure that no children in hospital go without a card, provide additional cards yourself – or have the children make extra cards.)

Making gifts for senior citizens

Is there a retirement home in the community, or an older person who lives alone near the school? Talk with the children about the loneliness that older people sometimes feel, and suggest some things that the children can do to cheer them up. Ask everyone to help you brainstorm a list of specific ideas, such as writing stories, drawing pictures, creating a book, performing a play, making figures out of modelling dough, or baking cakes. As a group, decide on at least one project to complete and deliver to older people in your area.

48

Make arrangements for the children to visit the retirement home (or the homes of those living alone) and deliver their gift. Describe to the children what you consider acceptable behaviour for the visit.

After the visit, encourage the children to talk about the experience, focusing on what it was like to do something nice for someone else.

4

Co-operating with others

Teaching children to work collaboratively and with consideration for others is the goal of this unit. Two primary benefits of learning to co-operate with others are that learning is enhanced and interpersonal relationships are improved.

Sculpt your body

Children work in pairs. One child assumes a pose in response to a word you select from the list below. (Write the word on the board and read it aloud.) The other child faces the first child and mirrors the pose. Make sure both children in each pair have an opportunity to assume both roles.

happy

a rabbit

sad

brave

a doughnut

a bird

soggy

hot

crisp

cold

excited

friendly

curious

polite

Sculpting with play dough

Have the children work in pairs to create a joint sculpture out of play dough. For a new twist on play dough, use this recipe for Peanut Play Dough.

You will need:
1/2 cup peanut butter
1/2 cup dried
skimmed milk
2/3 tablespoon honey

1. Mix the peanut butter and dry milk.
2. Add the honey.
3. Mix and knead until you achieve a good dough-like consistency.

Peanut Play Dough should be refrigerated in a covered container. It can be eaten, modelled, stretched, pounded and rolled; however, it does not harden well, so don't have the children keep their creations for very long.

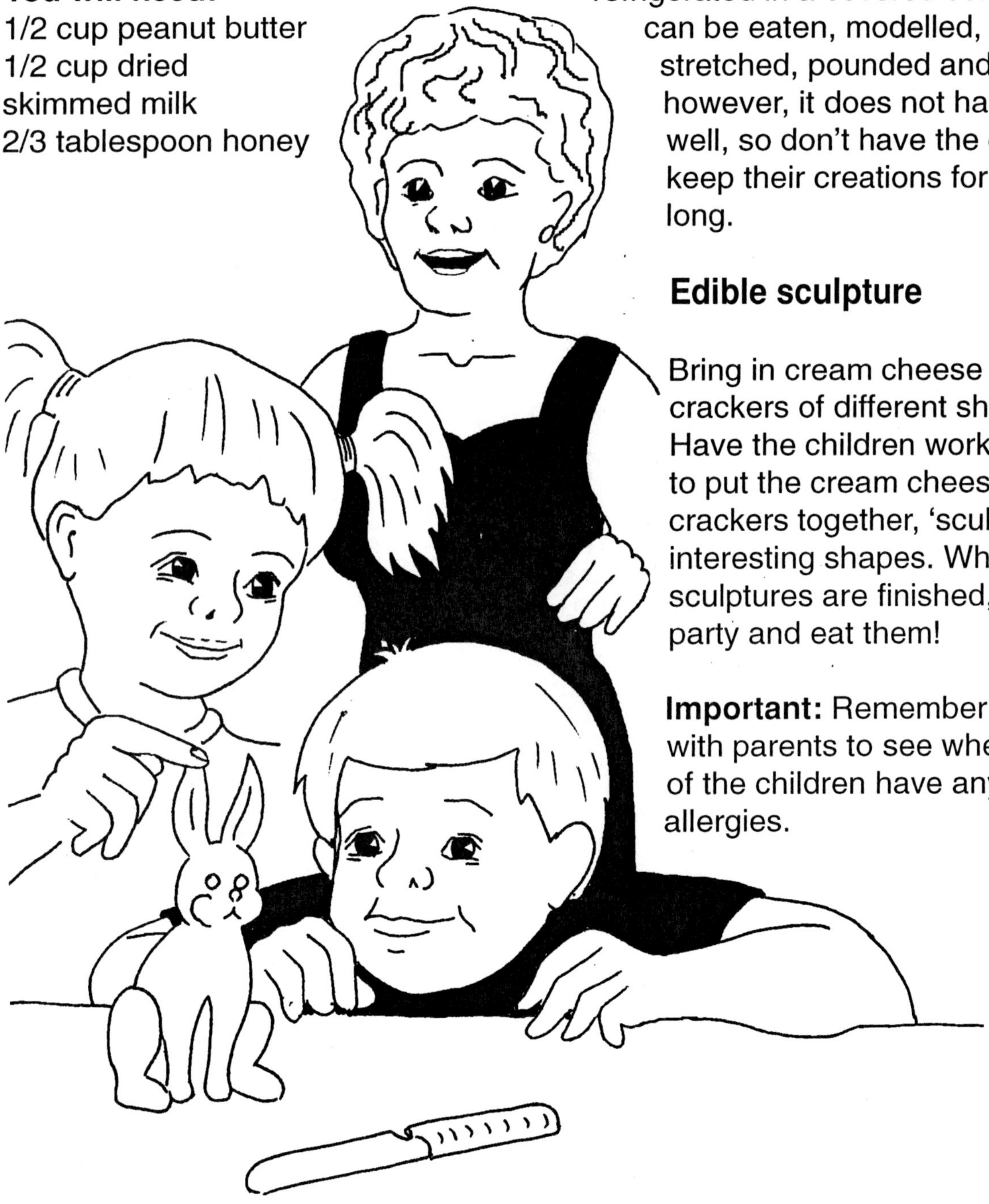

Edible sculpture

Bring in cream cheese and crackers of different shapes. Have the children work in teams to put the cream cheese and crackers together, 'sculpting' interesting shapes. When the sculptures are finished, have a party and eat them!

Important: Remember to check with parents to see whether any of the children have any food allergies.

Communication co-operation

Bring in a 'pin-the-tail-on-the-donkey' game or make one of your own on large paper. If you make your own game, try a new twist, such as 'pin-the-collar-on-the-dog', 'pin-the-saddle-on-the-horse', or 'pin-the-ball-on-the-seal's-nose'.

Have the children work in pairs. One child gives verbal directions to the other (who is blind-folded), using only words to guide the pinning of the object.

54

Two-person volleyball

Bring in enough round balloons that each team of two can have one. In place of a net, have each team use a chair. Follow normal volleyball procedures/rules, with one exception: have the children play on their knees. See which team can keep its balloon in the air the longest. After the game, talk with the children about specific teamwork behaviour involved in keeping the balloons up.

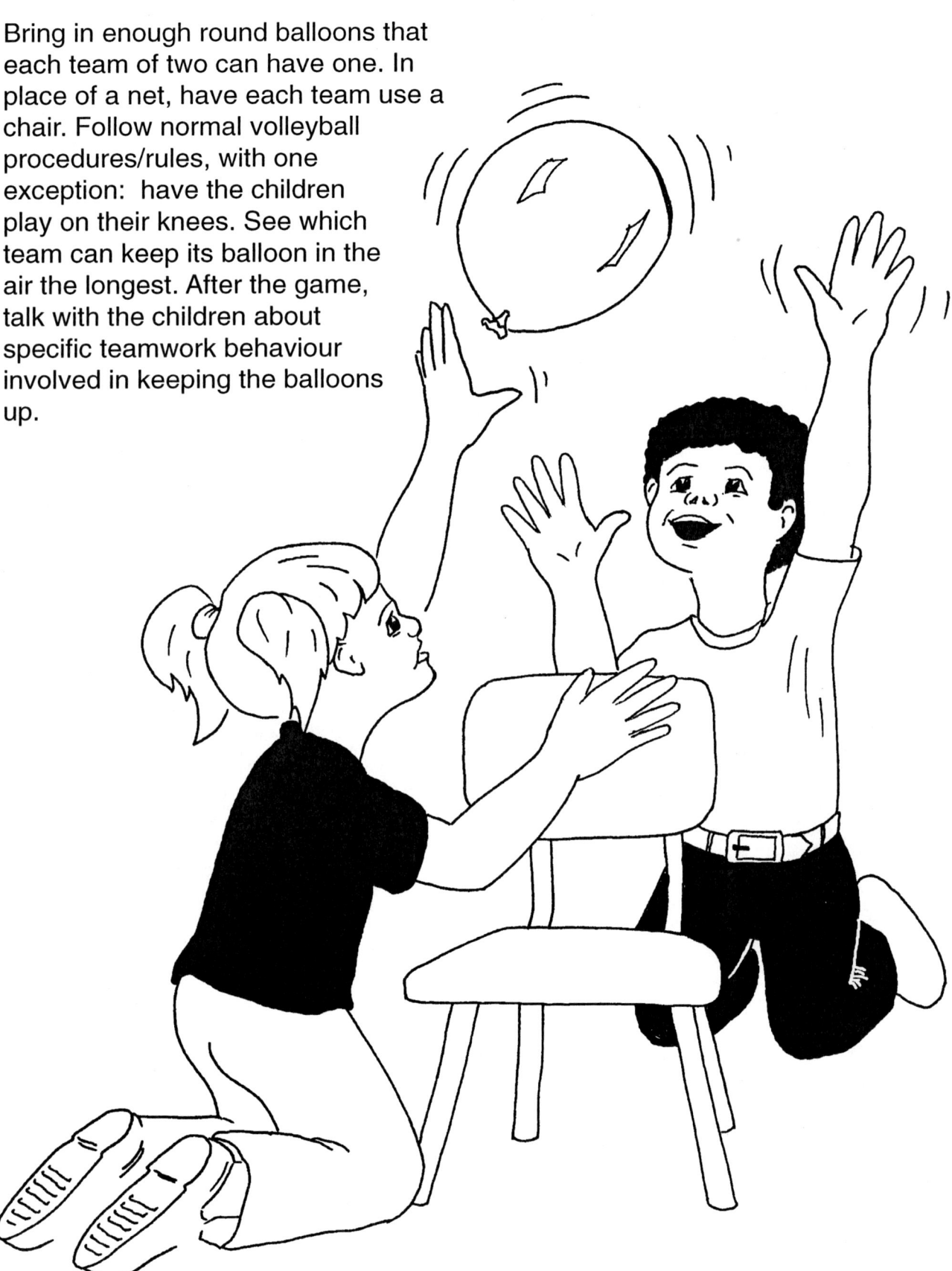

Co-operative dancing

Lead this movement activity to help children develop appreciation for the need to co-operate and stay 'in tune' with others. Ask the children to bring in shoe boxes (you'll need two for each child). With each foot in a shoe box, have the children slide across the floor as you play a slow musical selection. Then ask the children to dance with a partner. Again, accompany the dancing with a slow musical selection. Have the children move around the floor in time with the music and in step with each other.

Play several musical selections. With each selection, choose a slightly more upbeat tempo. Finish the dancing with a lively, quick number. Remind the children to continue to dance together, in complementary rhythm. After the dancing, ask the children: 'What was it like to dance alone?' 'What was it like to dance with someone else?' 'What did you do to keep in tune with each other?'

Our class newspaper

Make a giant newspaper. Near the top of a large sheet of heavy paper, print 'Our Class'. Explain that this *headline* tells what the stories and pictures in the newspaper will be about. Assist the children in writing or dictating stories about activities in which the class has been involved, as well as activities/experiences of individual children. Ask volunteers to draw pictures illustrating the different stories. Each month make a new page to add to the newspaper. Help the children decide on new *features* (story titles) for each issue. Display the newspaper throughout the year and share it with visitors.

Loving	Friendly	Helping
Happy	Sharing	Smiling
Giving	Caring	Understanding

Friendly words

Talk with the children about what *friendliness* and *understanding* mean to them. Ask the children to think of words that encourage friendliness and understanding between people. List the words that they suggest on the board (loving, sharing, giving, helping, happy, etc.).

A basket of friendly flowers

Have each child draw and cut out five circles with flower petal shapes around each circle, and then paste stems of different lengths on the flower shapes. Next, have them cut a basket shape from 9 x 12cm sugar paper and paste the five flowers behind the basket. Now, ask them to select five friendly words from the list on the board, writing one word on each flower. Place the baskets of friendly flowers around the room.

58

Working together

Find pictures of people working together. Possibilities include: workers on a construction site, a family preparing dinner together, people working together in an office. Show the pictures to the children and ask them to identify and discuss what the people in the pictures are doing. Encourage discussion by asking questions such as: 'Are these people helping each other?' 'Are they working together to get the job done? Why?' 'If you were in this picture, what would you be doing to help?' 'Do you like to help other people?'

Have the children each bring in a picture of people working together, or have them cut pictures out of old magazines that you provide. One at a time, go through the pictures and ask the children to decide if the picture shows a job that one person can do alone or a job that requires two or more people. Encourage the children to explain their decisions.

When children bring in items such as toys or books to share, use the opportunity to discuss with the entire class the feelings and pleasures derived from sharing with others.

59

What are rules for?

A good way to help children develop an understanding of rules and the necessity of having them is to involve them in a discussion. Begin by eliciting their comments about seemingly unnecessary rules that adults force children to obey. List the rules that they come up with, and discuss them one at a time. Allow the children to express any feelings they have relative to each rule; then talk about what it would be like if that rule didn't exist. Ask questions such as, 'What would the school (community, etc.) be like if we didn't have this rule?'

Have each child pick one school rule and create a poster depicting the rule.

What do I do?
Where do I do it?

This activity helps children to determine which actions are appropriate in specific settings and situations.

Show pictures representing the following places: school, church, park, garden, bedroom, living room, kitchen, busy street, supermarket, pavement. Have the children identify and discuss the settings. Ask them to name an activity that they might observe in each of the different places. Then, ask them to name activities that would be inappropriate in each setting. Finally, read the following words, one at a time, and ask the children to name suitable settings for each action: *run, yell, sing, walk, play, sleep, dance, sit quietly, eat, swing, laugh.*

In a hurry?

Read to the class a version of Aesop's fable 'The Hare and the Tortoise'. After the story, encourage discussion by asking these and other questions: 'When is it necessary to hurry?' 'When is it all right to get in front of someone?' 'When is it not safe or necessary to hurry?' 'Why do you think people queue up?' 'When is it unnecessary for people to queue up?'

Responsibility

To develop the children's sense of responsibility to others, discuss the importance of being on time. Demonstrate the concept by using a clock with moveable hands or a paper-plate clock that you have made (see Directions for making a clock).

Place the hands of the clock to show different times that things happen each day, such as the time school begins, lunch time, and the end of the school day. Ask the children to show the time they go to bed or the time of their favourite TV programme, or the time they get up in the morning. Discuss why clocks are needed, and talk about what it means to be late. Ask questions like: 'Were you ever late?' 'What happened?' 'How did the people who were waiting for you feel?' 'What do you think would happen if your father or mother were late for work every day?' 'What would happen if your teacher were late?' or 'What would happen if a doctor or ambulance were late getting to a person who needed help?'

Have the children draw a picture or write a story about a real or imaginary incident in which they were late.

Directions for making a clock

Materials needed:
paper plate
paper fastener
highlighter pen
1 sheet heavy sugar paper

Indicate the hours with a highlighter around the outside edge of the paper plate. Cut out big and little hands from sugar paper. Attach one end of each hand to the centre of the paper plate with a single fastener. Make sure that the holes in the hands are large enough for the hands to rotate around the fastener.

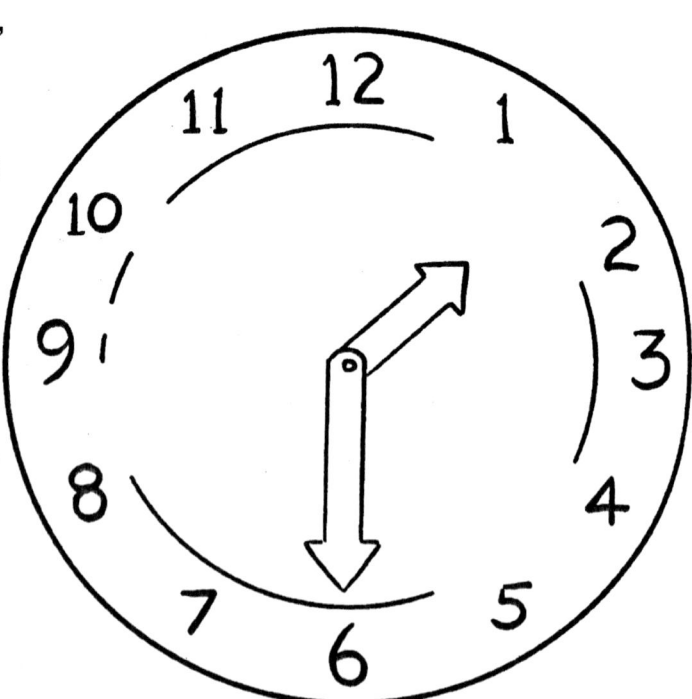

Let's have a party

A good way to provide children with an experience in co-operation is to give a party. Invite another class to be your guests. Before the party, have the children co-operate in making refreshments, setting the refreshment table, and cleaning and decorating the room, as necessary. When the other class arrives, the children can serve the food. After the party, they can clear up. Help the children to understand that everyone's work is easier when people do their part and co-operate.

Easy classroom refreshments

Various sandwiches:
Have the children use biscuit cutters to make different shapes. Arrange attractively on a plate.

Biscuits:
Have the children spread icing on plain biscuits and make 'biscuit sandwiches'.

Punch:
Use bottled squash that only requires the addition of water.

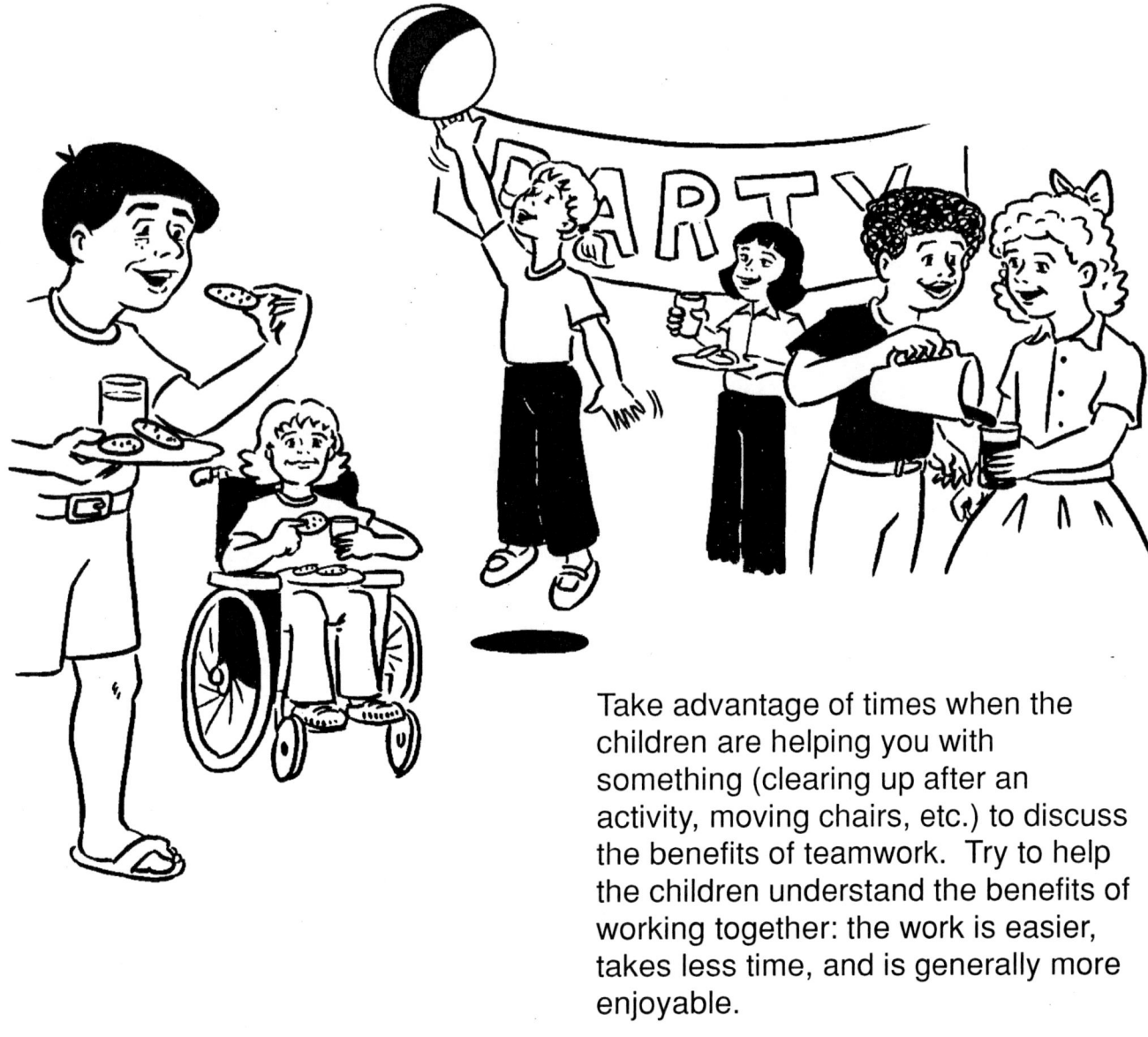

Take advantage of times when the children are helping you with something (clearing up after an activity, moving chairs, etc.) to discuss the benefits of teamwork. Try to help the children understand the benefits of working together: the work is easier, takes less time, and is generally more enjoyable.

5

My health and safety

The foundation for many lifelong health and lifestyle habits is established during the early years. This unit is designed to promote the development of healthy behaviours, and to give the children knowledge of positive actions to take in emergency situations.

How to stay well

Help the children develop the understanding that they can do many things on a regular basis to stay healthy, and that they are responsible for taking care of themselves.

Ask the children to name something they do to contribute to their own health and wellbeing. Be sure to contribute things that you do for yourself, too. Write suggestions on the board or on paper. Examples are: 'I eat fresh fruit and vegetables every day'. 'I brush my teeth regularly'. 'I get plenty of sleep each night'. 'I wash my hands before I eat', 'When it is cold, I put on warm clothes before going outside'. Provide art materials and have the children draw pictures of themselves doing healthy things.

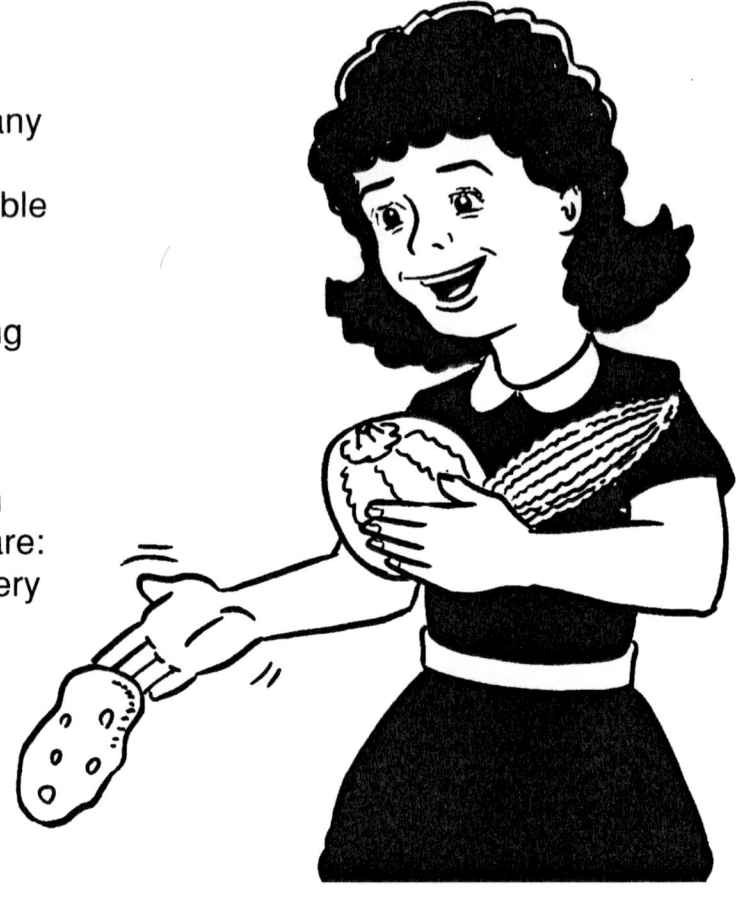

What's for lunch?

Help the children to develop an understanding of what constitutes a balanced meal. Provide plenty of magazines, particularly ones that have an abundance of food advertisements. Have the children cut out all the food items they can find. Have each child select several items to 'serve' at a meal. Discuss with individual children the items they have chosen. Point out which items are healthy (fruits, vegetables, cereals, etc.) and which should be eaten in moderation (fats, sweets, soft drinks, etc.). When all the children have selected a balanced meal, ask them to draw a place-setting on a large sheet of paper and paste their food items onto the paper.

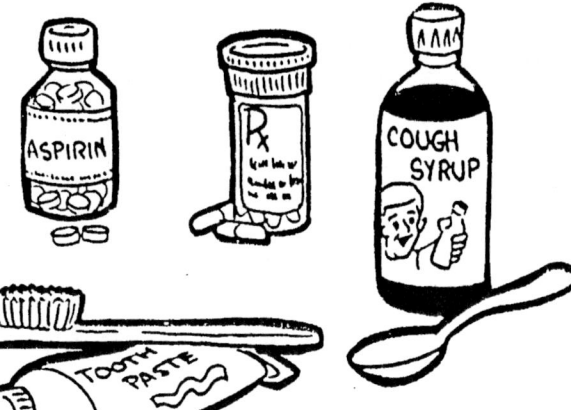

Where is the danger?

Some of the most important safety practices a child can learn have to do with avoiding dangerous substances. Bring in a number of empty bottles and boxes for toxic chemicals, poisons, medicines, etc. Bring in healthy items, too. Pick up one container at a time and discuss it with the children. Ask the children to help you identify containers for dangerous substances. Talk about how such containers should be handled. Describe the dangers of misuse, particularly the danger of swallowing. If the substance is not dangerous, ask the children how they might use it.

Some suggested items:

bleach	milk
first-aid cream	peanut butter
glue	sweets
iodine	pickles
fertilizer	biscuits
aspirin	crackers
wine	lemonade
cigarettes	tinned fruit
detergent	cleaning fluid
tinned vegetables	ink
prescription medicine	cough syrups

Whose house is this?

Help the children grasp the importance of knowing vital information concerning themselves and their families, especially in emergency situations. Emphasize that the children should always be able to provide their full name and address. Go around the room and have each child recite his/her name and address by saying, 'My name is _____ and I live at _____.' Provide art materials and have each child draw a picture of his/her house. In large letters, print the address at the bottom of the picture. Put the houses along one wall and play an identification game. Read the addresses, one at a time, and ask, 'Whose house is this?' The owner responds with his or her name and 'I live at _____,' repeating the address.

Using the phone for emergencies

Talk with the children about what might constitute an emergency. Point out that, when people really need help fast, they can dial 999. Bring in two telephones for a realistic demonstration. Role-play for the children by dialling 999 and reporting an emergency. Demonstrate good telephone habits.

Talk with the children about the importance of using good telephone habits – especially if they are providing emergency information over the phone. Stress that the children should speak clearly and loudly enough for the listener to hear everything, and that they should keep their statements short and to the point. Remind the children to stay on the line and be prepared to answer questions.

Discuss and demonstrate the correct way to hold a telephone while talking. Then, two at a time, have the children role-play emergency phone situations. Provide some situations which require emergency action using the phone. One child dials 999 and reports the emergency, while the other child listens and asks questions.

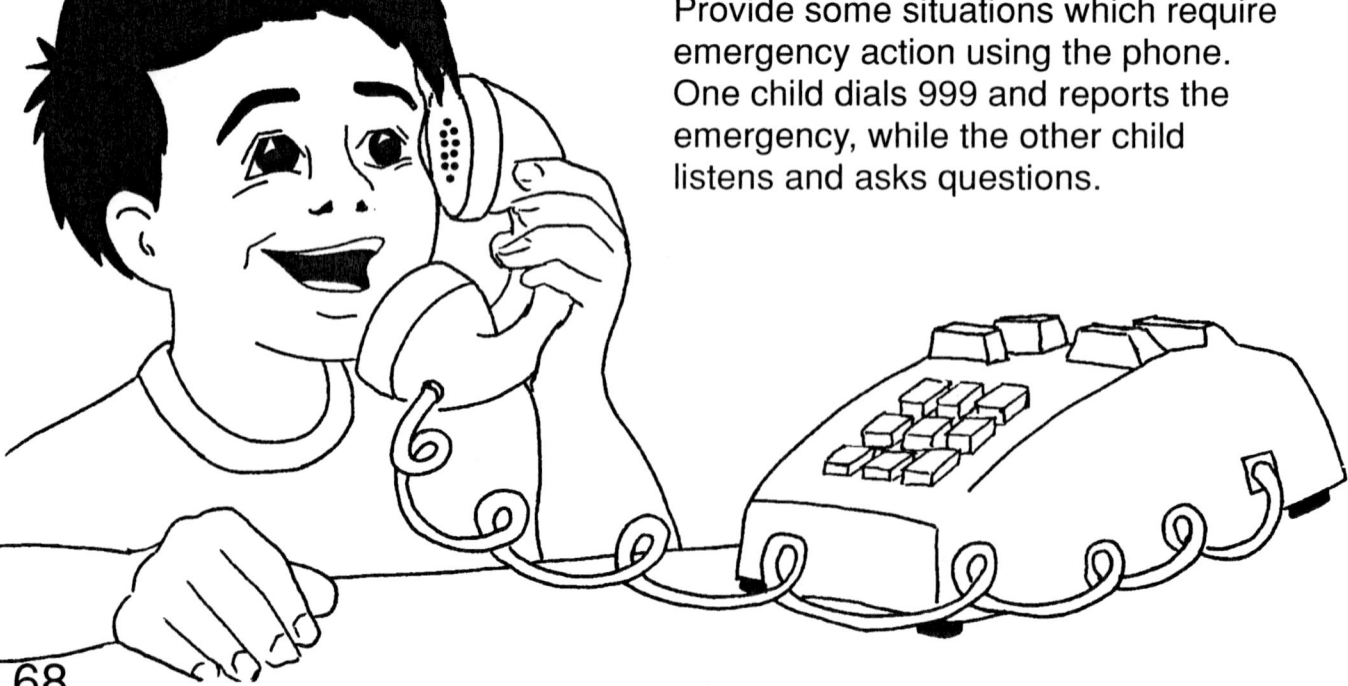

An 'Emergency' game

Present a variety of hypothetical situations posing different kinds of emergencies. Discuss positive ways to handle each situation. Explain that, in this game, the children are to analyze each emergency and then decide on the best way to handle it.

Some examples are:
- You are home alone. A water pipe bursts and is leaking water all over the dining room carpet.
- You are taking a walk in the woods along a narrow path. Stretched out ahead of you is a snake.

- You go home after school, nobody is at home, and you realize you have forgotten your key.
- You wake in the middle of the night, look out of your bedroom window, and see flames coming out of your neighbour's house.
- You come home from school and notice that the door is open. Nobody is supposed to be at home.
- You and your friend are walking home from school in the rain when someone you don't know offers to give you a lift.
- You are home alone and a stranger comes to the door.
- You wake up in the middle of the night and hear someone in your back garden.
- You are home alone when you start to feel very sick. Your head aches, your stomach is upset, and you have hot and cold chills.
- While you are using the electric toaster, sparks and smoke start to come from the socket.

Books available to reinforce this practice; *Safety first* (Heinemann First Library), *Stay Safe* (Wayland), *Look out series* RoSPA (Evans Brothers Ltd)

Who helps?

From magazines, books, and posters, make a display of pictures of emergency services personnel. Include a firefighter, police officer, 'lollipop' person, paramedic, and school nurse, plus any others you can locate. Present these and additional situations and ask the children which of the emergency staff would assist in each situation:

- A fire breaks out in a house on your road.
- A car crash occurs nearby.
- A teenager is hit by a car.
- There is a break-in at the DIY store.
- Young children need help crossing the road in front of the school.
- Someone breaks into and vandalizes the school.
- A dog bites a child in the school playground.

After discussing a number of situations, have the children role-play the situations.

Invite one or more emergency services personnel to visit your classroom. Ask each to make a presentation on the role he/she plays in helping the community to remain safe. Or if possible visit one or more places where emergency services personnel work, such as a police station or fire station.

A fire drill

Discuss with the children the importance of fire drills and why a quick evacuation of a building is so important in a fire. Practise an emergency evacuation with the children.

Ask the children to help you draw a floor plan of the school on a large sheet of chart paper. Put in all rooms, doors, and windows. Walk through the building and note the exit signs and put them on your floor plan, too. (This would be a good time to remind the children that it is always wise to note the exit sign in any building they enter.)

On the floor plan, draw a line from your classroom through the nearest exit door to the outside. Discuss what doors the children should use should a fire start when they are not in the classroom. Walk through the building and identify the various exit doors that serve different parts of the school complex.

'Sign' language

Talk with the children about the importance of signs and that they provide lots of helpful information. Often they warn us of danger, keep traffic running smoothly, or keep us going in the right direction. Take the children on a walk around the neighbourhood and look for signs. Notice what types of signs you see, what colour and shape they are, etc. Stop and read as many as you can and discuss their value and why they have been placed where they have. You might like to keep a tally of the different types of signs that you see, such as traffic signs, pedestrian signs, signs associated with private property and directional signs. When you return to the classroom, have the children suggest signs that might be useful in the classroom. Provide art material and have the children make the signs and place them around the room.

Traffic safety

Use this activity to teach traffic safety and the importance of safety regulations. This activity also helps children develop good attitudes toward this aspect of law enforcement.

Direct the children to construct a grid of 'streets' in an open area of the classroom, using books, tables, chairs, and other moveable objects. Create different types of traffic signs and signals out of sugar paper, using the correct colours and shapes. Have the children take on the roles of police officer, car driver, bus driver, and pedestrians. Discuss the safety regulations represented by the various signs, and then have the children dramatize different situations that involve drivers, pedestrians, and the emergency services.

A smaller, tabletop layout of streets can be created by using toy cars, trucks, and dolls.

Making a first aid kit

Provide, or have each child bring in, the following materials:

- shoe box
- glue
- paint
- ribbon (in lengths long enough to tie around a shoe box)
- assorted first aid supplies:
  - plasters, gauze, tape, cotton wool, antiseptic lotion, and antiseptic cream

Explain to the children that they will be making first aid boxes to take home. Begin by having the children paint their shoe boxes, being sure to write 'First Aid Kit' on top. When the paint dries, have the children glue the ribbon to the bottom of the box, allowing enough length on both ends of the ribbon to tie around the box. As the children fill their boxes with the first aid supplies, discuss each item and how and when it might be used. Ask the children where at home they might place their first aid kit so that everyone will have easy access to it.

Note: You might like to send a note to parents explaining that the children have made first aid kits as part of a unit on personal health and safety. Suggest that parents hold a family discussion, talking about the use of the kit and deciding on a good place to keep it.

Five boxes for five senses

Talk with the children about the five senses and how they are used. Ask the children to imagine what it would be like to lose one of their senses. Provide five boxes, each labelled with one sense: touch, sight, smell, taste, and hearing. Collect items that can be readily identified with one of the senses and put them in the appropriate box. Examples are: *Touch* – sandpaper, cotton wool, a marble, sponge. *Sight* – items of various colours, shapes, and sizes. *Smell* – liquorice, mint leaves, cinnamon stick, garlic clove, perfume-soaked cotton wool. *Taste* – a variety of foods, including sweet, sour, and salty (e.g. crackers, crisps, raw fruit, and sweets). *Hearing* – bell, rattle, squeaky toy, marbles in a small tin box, cellophane paper, bubble wrap.

Have the children work in small groups to experience and describe the items in each box. Pass the boxes among the groups. When a group has the touch box, instruct the members to take turns touching different items, describe each item to other members of the group, and then remove the item from the box for all to see. When the group has the sight box, have the members remove one item at a time, place it on top of the box, and describe it. For the smell box, have the children close their eyes and smell one item at a time. For the hearing box, ask them to create a noise inside the box with one item at a time. Before doing the taste box, make sure that the children wash their hands. Have them place one food item at a time inside the box. The children should close their eyes when tasting and describing each item.

Caring for the environment

Rachel Carson was a biologist, writer and ecologist who died in 1964. The four books she wrote are still in print and available today. In her book, *The Sense of Wonder*, Rachel Carson writes that it is more important to begin with *feelings* about the natural world than with knowledge of it and she details her philosophy that adults need to nurture a child's inborn sense of wonder about the natural world.

The activities in this unit are designed to inspire these feelings of wonder in young children. Also included are activities that allow children to develop an understanding of critical issues central to the environmental movement and how they can be involved in affecting their immediate environments – home, school, and community.

What do plants need to grow?

Help the children to understand that all plants and animals on earth contribute to the balance of nature. Each plant and animal has a job to do, and everything in the environment is connected in important ways. All people and animals depend on plants to purify the air they breathe. Plants take in the carbon dioxide that animals and people breathe out, and turn it into oxygen, which animals and people then breathe in.

Ask the children to name all the things a plant needs to be healthy (sun, water, soil, air, etc.). Then, have them name items people need to be healthy (food, water, air, shelter, etc.). Write the items down as the children list them. Discuss with the children the similarities and differences.

Plant uses

Cut pictures of plants out of magazines. Discuss with the children some of the ways in which plants help people (food, building materials, shade, beauty, etc.) and some of the ways in which people help plants (cultivation, fertilization, pruning, elimination of pests, etc.). Show the different pictures to the children and ask them to name some ways in which people might use each plant.

Bean pictures

Provide a variety of dried beans and seeds, as well as glue and heavy paper or cardboard. Have the children draw a picture on their paper or cardboard and then 'paint' the picture by glueing the beans and seeds onto the surface of the drawing. Preserve the pictures with a clear plastic spray or a light coat of varnish.

Plant a seedling

Provide seedlings, large paper cups, and potting soil. Write each child's name on a paper cup. Have the children choose a seedling and plant it in their cup with some soil. Talk about all the things that trees are used for, and discuss the importance of using natural resources wisely and of replacing what is used.

Place the seedlings in a sunny place and have the children water them as needed. Encourage the children to note any growth or changes. After caring for the plants in the classroom for a while, encourage the children to take their seedlings home and plant them.

This is an excellent activity to coincide with The Tree Councils 'National Tree Week' (in November/December). Explain to the children that this day is a time to appreciate trees for their usefulness and beauty, and that it originated from the day when new trees were planted to remember loved ones lost in the war.
See www.treecouncil.org.uk

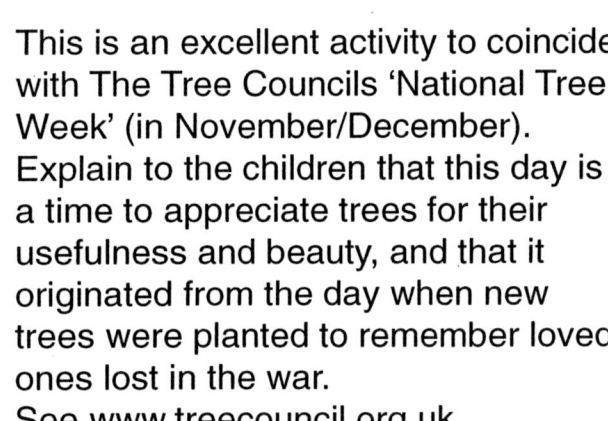

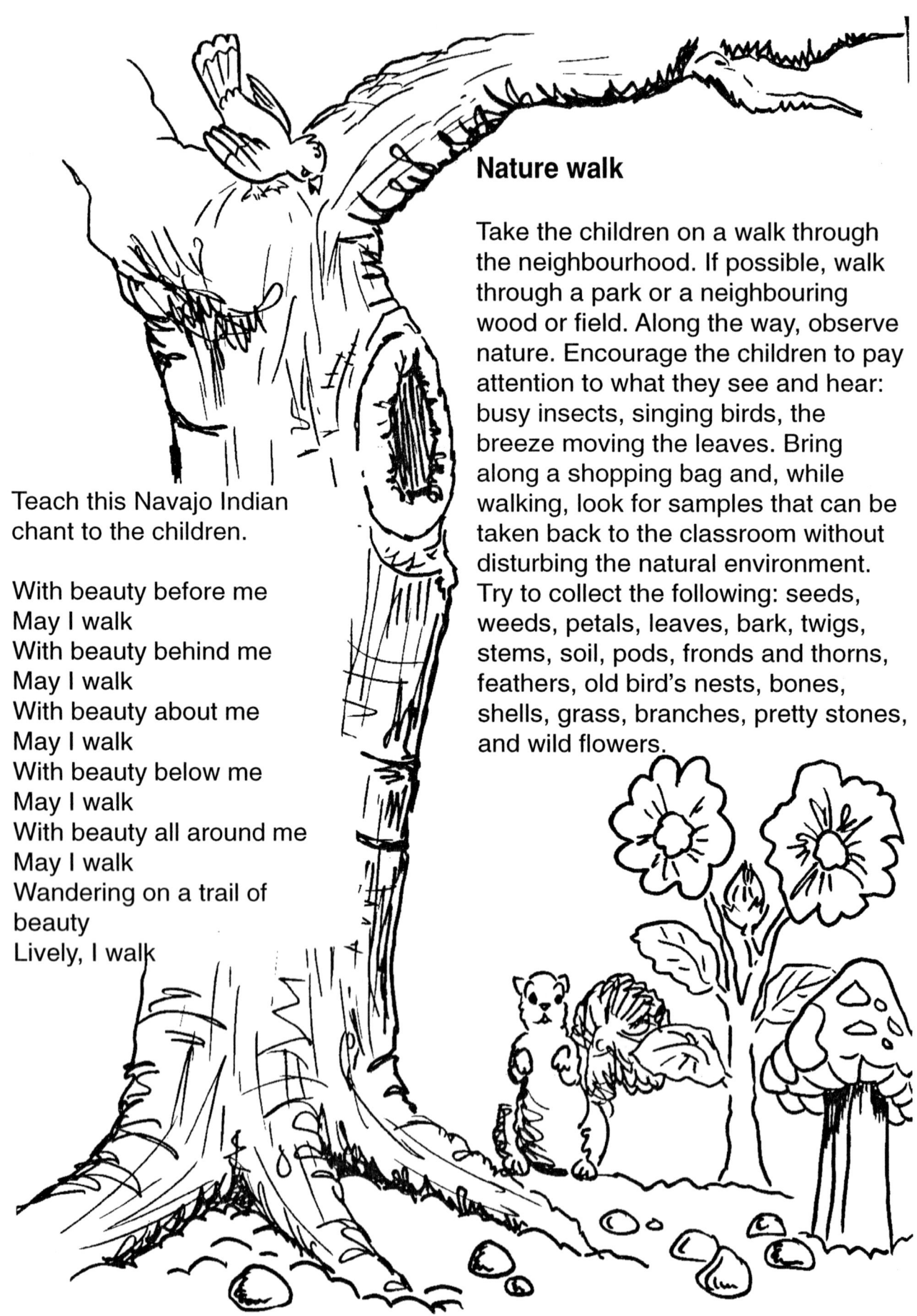

Nature walk

Take the children on a walk through the neighbourhood. If possible, walk through a park or a neighbouring wood or field. Along the way, observe nature. Encourage the children to pay attention to what they see and hear: busy insects, singing birds, the breeze moving the leaves. Bring along a shopping bag and, while walking, look for samples that can be taken back to the classroom without disturbing the natural environment. Try to collect the following: seeds, weeds, petals, leaves, bark, twigs, stems, soil, pods, fronds and thorns, feathers, old bird's nests, bones, shells, grass, branches, pretty stones, and wild flowers.

Teach this Navajo Indian chant to the children.

With beauty before me
May I walk
With beauty behind me
May I walk
With beauty about me
May I walk
With beauty below me
May I walk
With beauty all around me
May I walk
Wandering on a trail of beauty
Lively, I walk

Things to do with samples from nature walks:

Make a mobile:

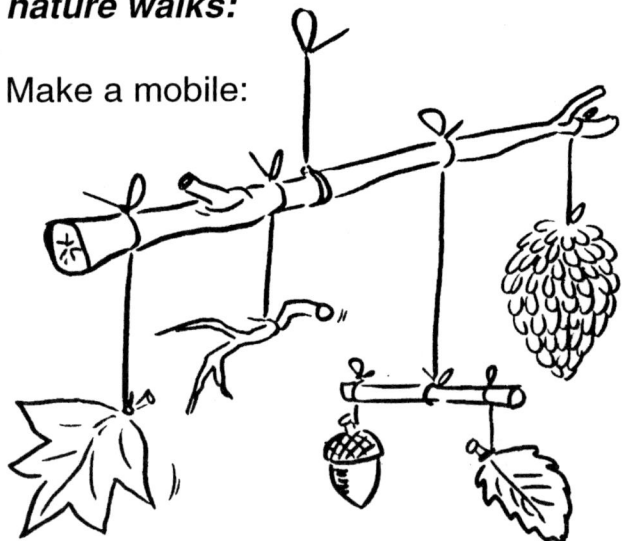

Have each child select one sample. Help the children glue their object to a piece of sugar paper. Then, have them draw or paint other details around the object, completing a picture of their own design. For example, they might draw a tree to complete a leaf, or a bird to complete a feather.

Press the flowers and leaves between two sheets of waxed paper placed between the pages of a heavy book. When dry, name and label the items and make a bulletin-board display.

Using an old shoe box, create a 'nature environment'. Place the open top of the box facing out, with one side of the box on the bottom. Place some of the soil you collected on the bottom, and arrange other samples around the box to create the desired scene.

Sort the samples according to colour. Ask the children to determine how many different colours are represented, and then to notice the variances within each colour. Prepare a chart for each colour. At the top of each chart, write the name of the colour followed by the word _like_. Beneath the heading, glue the different objects representing that colour and write what each object is. Display the charts around the room.

Spray-paint branches, tie them together with an attractive ribbon, and use the arrangement as a door or wall hanging.

Lovely as a tree

This activity allows children to observe and record perceptions of nature while teaching the meaning of co-operation and sharing.

Make one copy of the tree on the next page for every two children. Take the children for a walk to a nearby area where they can see several trees. Have the children select one tree and observe it in detail. Ask them to touch and describe the bark. Pick a leaf and pass it around, noticing its colour, texture, size, shape, etc. Look at the tree as a whole. What does it look like? What is its shape? How tall is it? How wide? Look at the tree from different angles – standing up, crouching down, lying on the ground. Discuss with the children what they are observing. Return to the class and have pairs of children work together, sharing one box of markers or crayons. Ask the children to make their illustrated tree look as much as possible like the real one they observed. When the pictures are complete, ask the children to describe how the tree looked to them. Write their descriptions on the board.

Adopt a tree

Take a walk in the school grounds or neighbourhood. Ask the children to take particular notice of all the trees, because you would like them to pick one special tree to 'adopt'. Spend some time at the tree. Notice what it looks like, take a measurement of its diameter, make bark rubbings, pick leaves off the ground and bring them back to the classroom. Have the children draw pictures of the tree. Return to the tree regularly and try to incorporate it into activities such as the ones just described.

Organic gardening in the classroom

Discuss with the children the elements that plants must have to grow (sunlight, air, water, and soil). Explain that the soil provides support for the plant as well as storing moisture and nutrients. Talk about the differences between healthy, well-nourished soil and poor soil in which plants don't grow healthy and strong. Talk about how farmers keep their soil healthy. Mention that many people make compost for their garden. Explain that the benefits of using compost are twofold: compost builds healthy, rich soil while providing a means for recycling organic waste.

Provide the following materials: a large tin or jar; assorted materials that are easily decomposed, such as coffee grounds, shredded newspaper, fruit rinds and skins, dried leaves and grass, and crushed cereal – all broken into small pieces. Have the children layer all the items into the tin. Stir the mixture and moisten with water. Cover the tin and punch several small holes in the top. Place it in a warm place and look at the contents daily. Every few days, stir the mixture. When everyone agrees that the mixture has turned to soil, plant some bean seeds in the tin. Place the tin in a sunny window, water regularly, and watch the plants grow.

Tending a mould garden

Discuss the use of mould in our environment.

Explain that, as a class, you are going to start a mould garden and are going to actually see the mould grow.

Bring in a piece of bread, a plate, and a glass jar large enough to cover the plate. Moisten the bread with only a few drops of water and place it on the plate. After about one hour cover the bread with the jar and place it in a dark place.

Look at the bread daily. Each day, observe the changes in the growth of the mould. Make a chart on which the children can record their daily observations.

How about an algae garden? Collect some rain water in a clear glass jar. Place it on a sunny windowsill. See how many days it takes for the water to turn green.

Pet rocks

This is a good activity to sharpen the children's appreciation of texture, shape, and colour in natural objects, and to make them aware that similar objects in nature have individual characteristics. Ask the children to look for rocks, to select one that they particularly like, and to bring that rock to school.

On a table, place a bowl of water, a scrubbing brush, and paper towels for washing and drying the rocks. Also provide a magnifying glass, and sandpaper to smooth any heavy caked areas. Have the children carefully examine their rocks both before and after cleaning. Invite them to use the magnifying glass. As they work with their rocks, encourage the children to discuss their observations. Ask questions such as: 'What are the colours in your rock?' 'What does it feel like to the touch?' 'What causes it to feel like that?' 'How did your rock change when you washed it?' 'How is your rock the same as someone else's?' 'How is it different?' Write each child's name on a piece of masking tape and attach it to his/her rock. Display the rocks together on a table. Have each child write a paragraph describing his/her rock.

For the birds

Create a display of bird pictures, books, and any nests or feathers that you can provide. Invite the children to join you in examining and discussing the items. Play a game with the children by making statements to which the children respond 'It's a bird' to any statement that says something true about birds. Some suggestions are: 'It has two legs'. 'It has a beak,' 'It says meow,' 'It lives in a nest,' 'It has teeth,' 'It has feathers'.

With the children's help make a birdhouse from a heavy cardboard box, using glue to put the pieces together. Have the children make paper cut-outs of birds using the diagram on the next page. Have each child colour and cut out his/her own bird. For younger children, provide the birds already cut out. When finished, the birds and birdhouse may be displayed on the table with the other bird items.

Note: If you and the children want to place the birdhouse outside, weatherproof the exterior with a heavy coat of varnish.

Building a nest

If possible, bring in a bird's nest and examine it with the children. Discuss with the children all the different types of materials birds use to make their nests (dried grass, twigs, leaves, string, feathers, etc.). Take a walk with the children. Provide each child with a paper bag. Ask the children to find items that birds might use to make a nest, and put them in their bag. Upon returning to the classroom, give each child some clay to form the base for a nest. Then, like birds, have the children put their found objects onto the clay to make a nest.

Clay recipe
1 cup flour
1 cup salt
1 rounded teaspoon powdered alum (available from chemists and health food shops)

Mix all the ingredients and knead until the mixture reaches a clay-like consistency. To store for a few days, wrap in a wet cloth.

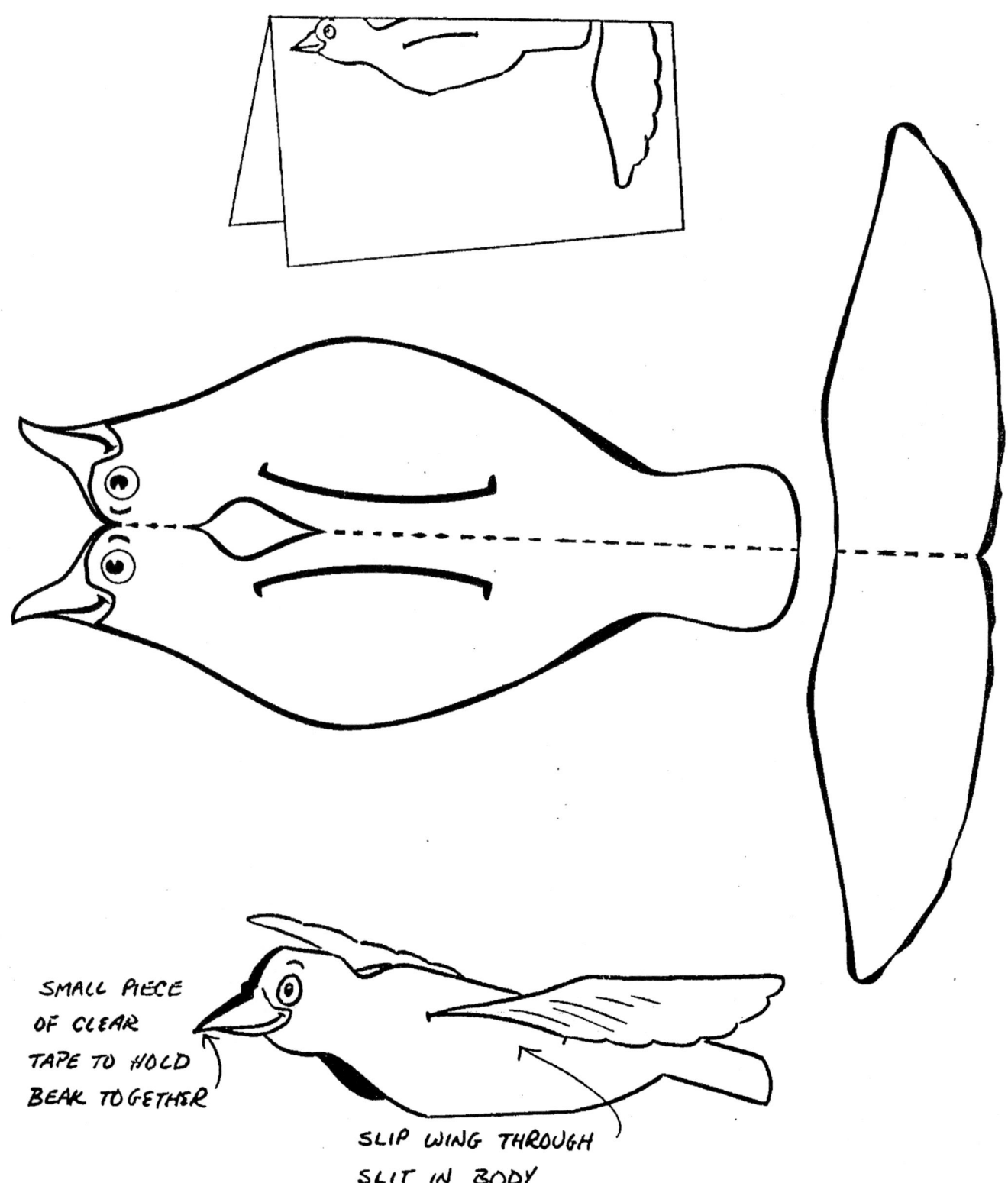

SMALL PIECE
OF CLEAR
TAPE TO HOLD
BEAK TOGETHER

SLIP WING THROUGH
SLIT IN BODY

The air we breathe

Talk with the children about how important it is to breathe clean air. Point out that, today, people have a great problem because car exhausts, factories, and power stations produce smoke, gases and dust that make the air dirty and polluted. Talk about how the breathing process works by discussing each of the following steps.

When you breathe in:
1. Your chest expands and your lungs fill with oxygen.
2. Blood cells inside your lungs absorb the oxygen.
3. Blood from the lungs goes to your heart.
4. Your heart pumps the blood throughout your body.
5. The oxygen in your blood cells helps keep your body healthy.

When you breathe out:
6. Your blood cells carry away carbon dioxide (CO_2) from all parts of your body.
7. The blood returns to your heart and the heart pumps it back to your lungs.
8. Your blood cells return the carbon dioxide to air inside your lungs.
9. Your chest is squeezed smaller and the air that is full of carbon dioxide is squeezed out.

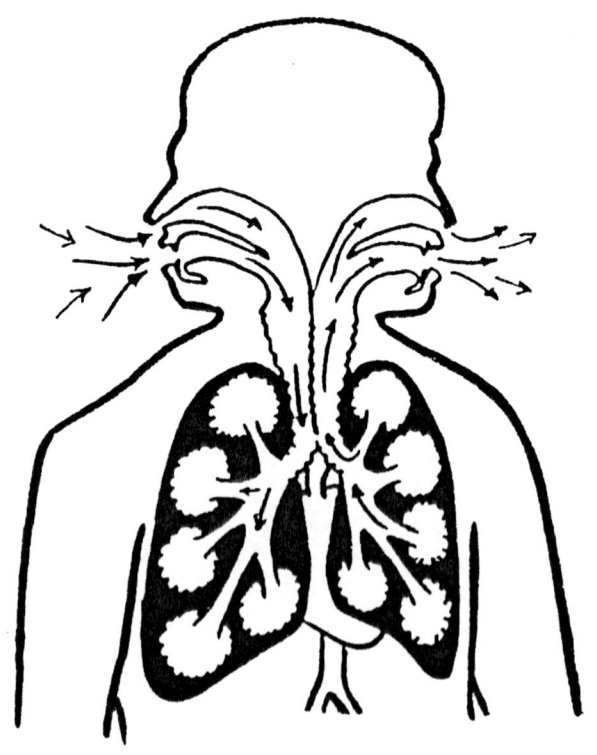

Do some breathing experiments

Using a clock with a second hand, have the children count the number of breaths they take in one minute. Next, have them run around the playground and immediately count their breaths again. Finally, ask the children to make a chart of their findings.

Find out how much air the lungs of the children can hold. Provide a large clear plastic bottle, 60cm of plastic tubing, a ruler or measuring tape, and a large bowl. Fill the bowl about one third full of water. Fill the plastic bottle to the top with water. Hold your hand over the bottle top and quickly turn the bottle upside down under the water in the bowl. Attach the ruler or measuring tape vertically to the side of the bottle and slip one end of the tube up inside the bottle. One at a time, have the children take a deep breath, hold their nose, and blow into the tube for as long as they can. Keep a record of how much water each child displaces from the bottle. This will give the children some idea of how much air they have in their lungs.

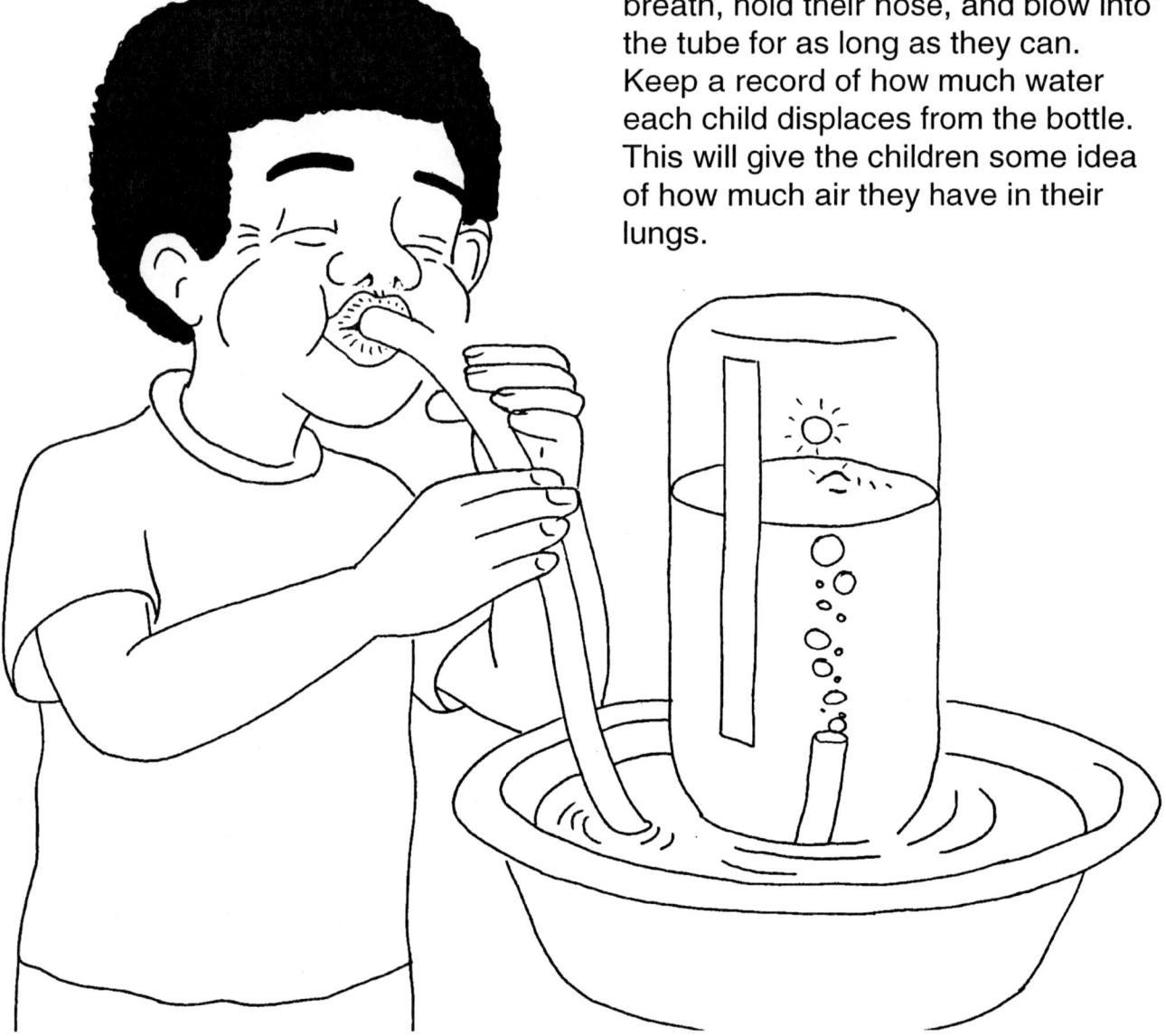

Catch the wind

Talk with the children about the fact that, although we hardly notice the air around us, it is the oxygen in the air we breathe that keeps us alive. Air is critical to our survival on a moment-to-moment basis. Explain that wind is the movement of the air around us. Watching the air turn a pinwheel provides an excellent demonstration of what wind movement can do.

Make a copy of the pinwheel pattern for each child. Also provide a plastic drinking straw, a straight pin, a small bead, tape, and crayons. Ask the children to colour both sides of their pinwheel pattern. Then have them cut on the solid line, being careful not to cut into the dotted line. Show the children how to fold and tape the corners as indicated in the directions. Next, push the pin through the centre of the pinwheel, through the bead, and then through the end of the plastic straw. **Caution:** Using pliers, bend the end of the pin down until it lies flat against the straw. Then tape the end of the straw, completely covering the end of the pin.

Have the children experiment with their pinwheels. Ask them to find out what happens when they blow the front …the back …the side. Take the pinwheels outside and have the children use them to judge how fast the wind is blowing.

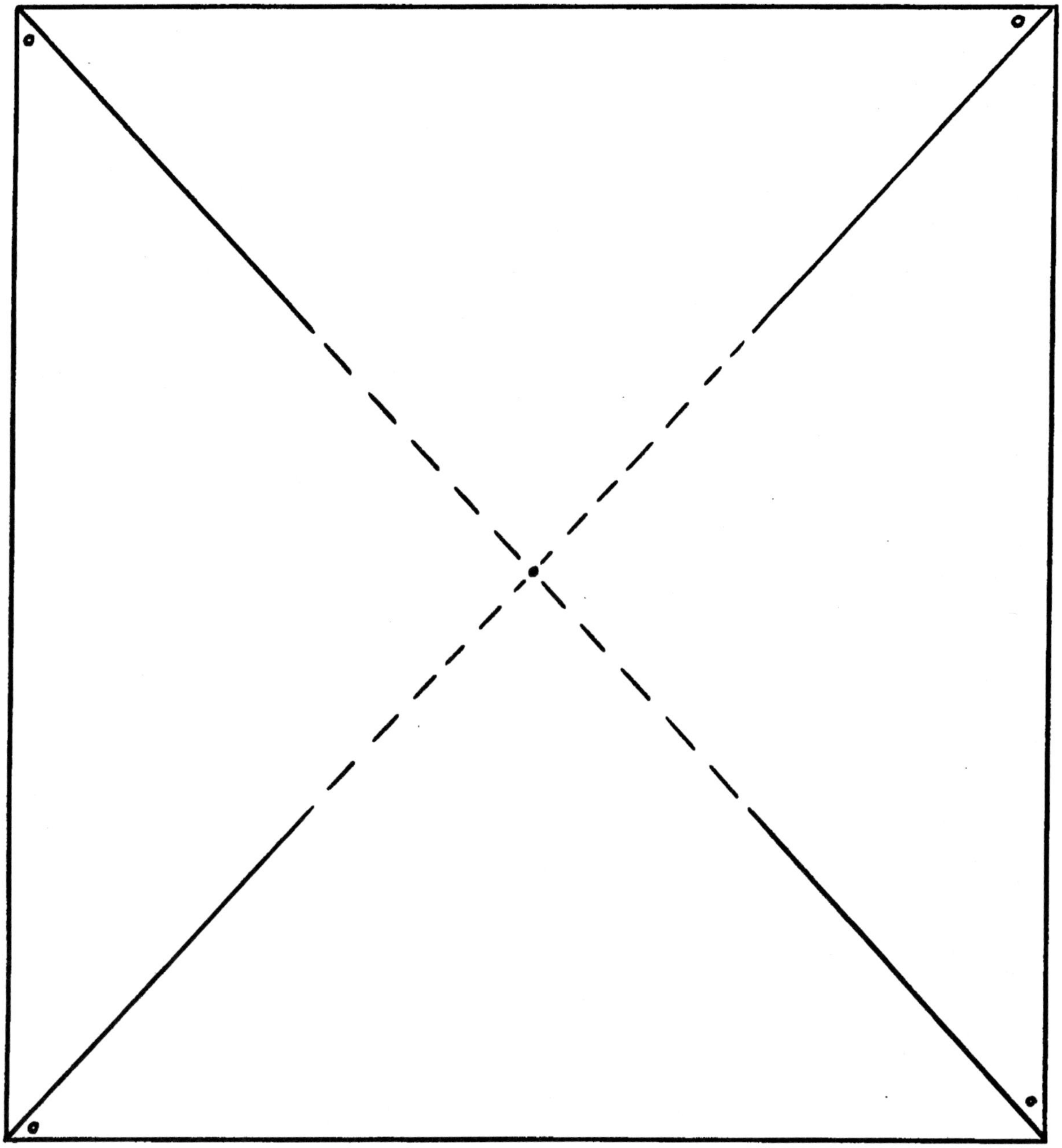

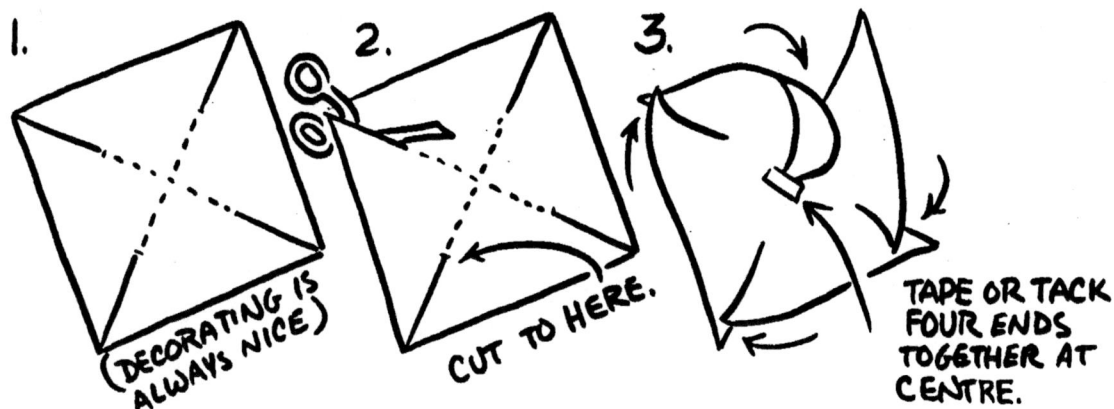

1.

(DECORATING IS ALWAYS NICE)

2.

CUT TO HERE.

3.

TAPE OR TACK FOUR ENDS TOGETHER AT CENTRE.

Learning about recycling

Help the children to become aware of the environment – why it is important to preserve and improve it, and how they can participate in caring for the earth through recycling. Bring in and display a number of items that are commonly recycled – a glass jar, aluminium can, plastic bottle, plastic shopping bag, newspaper, brown paper bag, corrugated box, grass clippings, etc. Ask the children if they can guess what all the items have in common. Give them time to consider a number of answers. If nobody gives the answer you are looking for, explain that these are items which are often recycled. Use this as a lead-in to a general discussion on ecology and the importance of recycling. Point out the following benefits of recycling.

Recycling saves space. When items are kept and re-used, fewer are discarded to end up in crowded dumps and bulging landfill sites.

Recycling saves energy. Less energy is required to recycle (melt aluminium cans, crush glass, convert newspaper into clean paper, etc.) than to make new products from raw materials.

Recycling saves resources. When we recycle, old materials are made into new products, so fewer raw materials are used. Recycling also helps to reduce air and water pollution.

Recycling survey

Have the children conduct a survey to learn about the recycling habits of their relatives, neighbours and classmates. Develop a questionnaire using these and/or other questions.

Do you currently recycle any of the following items?
1. aluminium cans
2. aluminium foil
3. glass jars and bottles
4. plastic bottles and tubs
5. plastic shopping bags
6. paper shopping bags
7. magazines
8. newspapers
9. telephone directories
10. cardboard boxes
11. computer paper
12. polystyrene foam food containers and trays

If you recycle or re-use, what are the reasons you do so?
1. I want to save energy.
2. I want to save money.
3. I want to save natural resources.
4. I want to prevent water and air pollution.
5. I can show my concern and commitment to the environment by recycling.

If you currently don't recycle or re-use, which statement best reflects your reasons:
1. I haven't really thought about it.
2. I don't know where a recycling centre is.
3. I don't have the time to recycle.
4. I don't have the space to recycle.
5. It's too much trouble.
6. I really don't care.

When the children return with their surveys, tally all the responses on a group chart. Use this to foster a discussion on what the children could do to assist others who are not doing so to recycle.

Litter lookout

Provide a definition of litter to the children, and talk about why everyone should be concerned about the litter problem. Litter is any unneeded item that has not been disposed of in a proper place. Litter takes away from the beauty of the environment and can cause illness and other health-related problems. For one week, ask the children to take note of all the litter they notice in places like the school playground, parks, neighbourhood, streets, and in their garden. Make a class litter chart. Each morning, put tally marks under all of the categories in which the children have seen litter.

Provide large sheets of paper and art materials, and have the children create anti-litter posters. Display the posters around the room or, if possible, throughout the school.

Energy audit

Most local power companies will conduct an energy audit free of charge. Invite a representative to audit your school or classroom and have him/her explain the findings to the children.

Figure this

Have the children research the answers to these questions:

Each person in the United Kingdom uses about 210kg of paper a year. In one year, what is the total amount of paper used in the United Kingdom?

Each year 25 billion Styrofoam cups are thrown away. If all of these cups were placed end to end in a line, how many times would the line circle the earth?

Be an environmental news reporter

Do this activity as a co-operative event by having the children work in teams of four.

Suggest to the children several areas of environmental concern. Have each group choose one on which to complete a news article. Possibilities include recycling, endangered species, pollution, ozone depletion, and renewable energy. Ask the children to do research by going to the library, asking questions, looking in newspapers and magazines for information, and checking TV listings for programmes related to their topic. Remind them that, as they are doing their research, they should look for answers to five important questions:

Who?
What?
Where?
When?
Why?

Ask the children to keep a notebook of all the things they learn. Give the children a couple of weeks to do their research and then have each group prepare and deliver a presentation to the rest of the class.

Environmental scrapbook

Bring in or make a scrapbook with large pages. Along with the children, collect interesting items on the environment. These should include: newspapers and magazine articles; pictures; interviews; facts, figures, charts, and graphs. Drawings and stories which the children have done can also be included. Be sure to gather good news about the environment as well as accounts of environmental problems. Allow the children to sort, arrange, and paste the items into the scrapbook. Have them create headings and add their own poetry, stories, and comments.

Printed in the United Kingdom
by Lightning Source UK Ltd.
103629UKS00001B/11-60